EXPLORE YOU

Also by John Young

The Case Against Christ (Hodder & Stoughton)
Creating Confidence in Evangelism (CPAS)
Jesus: The Verdict (Lion)
Know Your Faith (Hodder & Stoughton)
Practical Ideas in Evangelism (CPAS)
Teach Yourself Christianity (Hodder & Stoughton)

Explore Your Faith

Study Courses for Groups and Individuals

John Young

Hodder & Stoughton

LONDON SYDNEY AUCKLAND

To Kathleen, my mother, and to my grandchildren
Robert, Mary and Emma – with love,
gratitude and prayers.

Copyright © 1999 John Young

First published in Great Britain 1999

The right of John Young to be identified as the Author of
the Work has been asserted by him in accordance
with the Copyright, Designs and Patents Act 1988.

10 9 8 7 6 5 4 3 2 1

British Library Cataloguing in Publication Data
A record for this book is available from the British Library

ISBN 0 340 73540 6

Typeset by Avon Dataset Ltd, Bidford-on-Avon, Warks

Printed and bound in Great Britain by
Clays Ltd, St Ives plc

Hodder & Stoughton Ltd
A Division of Hodder Headline
338 Euston Road
London NW1 3BH

Contents

Preface

One welcome feature of modern church life is the growth in the number of groups which gather for fellowship, prayer and study. For some years I have been aware of the need for such groups to be served by material which informs and sparks lively discussion. It was for this reason that I wrote *Know Your Faith* (on the great themes of the Apostles' Creed) and added a study guide to *The Case Against Christ*.

And it was for this reason that my colleague Simon Stanley and I founded **York Courses** in 1996. Simon's background as a radio producer and parish priest means that we have been able to provide a number of audio-tape courses (for use in Lent or at other times) featuring several high-profile Christian leaders whose words appear in this volume. We are grateful to all the participants, especially the Archbishop of York and Steve Chalke who have participated more than once.

The response grows annually, and the most recent course was used by around 35,000 Christians, meeting in study groups from a wide range of churches. Thousands more heard extracts from the audio-tapes on local BBC radio stations.

The text of some of the courses has been carried in a remarkably wide range of national church newspapers: *Baptist Times*, *Catholic Herald*, *Church of England Newspaper*, *Methodist Recorder* and *War Cry*. This is an unusual and most encouraging indication of ecumenical co-operation, and I am extremely grateful to the editors for agreeing to go down this uncharted road.

When Hodder & Stoughton suggested that these courses might be gathered together in one book I was delighted to think that even more groups might have access to the material. And it provided a most welcome opportunity to include excellent courses from two colleagues whose work would otherwise be unknown to a wider public.

I am tremendously grateful to the Revd Ian Parkinson, Vicar of Saltburn, and Chris Woodcock, who is in great demand as a counsellor and trainer, for allowing me to edit and include their work. Their style and approach are different from mine, so this material adds a welcome variety to the mix.

While saying thank you, I wish to express my immense gratitude to Barbara Thompson for her commitment and for lending her unrivalled shorthand and typing skills to the production of this book.

Finally, a special thank you to Simon and Elaine Stanley for their unfailing friendship, laughter and dedicated labour, which gave birth to *York Courses* and hence, indirectly, to this book.

John Young
York

Suggestions for Group Leaders

1 **THE ROOM** Discourage people from sitting outside or behind the main circle – all need to be equally involved.

2 **HOSPITALITY** I suggest tea or coffee on arrival at the first meeting. Perhaps at the end too – to encourage folk to talk informally. Some groups might be more ambitious – taking it in turns to bring a dessert to start the evening (even in Lent, hospitality is OK!), with coffee at the end.

3 **THE GROUP**

    (a) *Getting under way* If group members do not know each other well some kind of 'icebreaker' might be helpful. You might invite people to share something quite secular (where they grew up, holidays, hobbies, significant object, etc.) or something more 'spiritual' (one thing I like and one thing I dislike about my church/denomination).

    (b) *Preparing the group* Take the group into your confidence, e.g. 'I've never done this before' **or** 'I've led lots of groups and every one has contained surprises'. Sharing vulnerability is designed to encourage *all* members to see the success of the group as their responsibility.

    • **Encourage** those who know that they talk easily, to ration their contributions. You might introduce a fun element by producing a bell which all must obey instantly.

    • **Encourage** the reticent to speak at least once or twice – however briefly. Explain that there are no 'right' answers and that among friends it's OK to say things that you are not sure about – to express half-formed ideas. But, of course, if individuals choose to say nothing, that is all right too.

4 **THE MATERIAL** In each session some questions are based on personal experience. You are advised to start with these.

Encourage members to read next week's chapter before the meeting, if possible.

Don't attempt to answer all questions – a lively exchange of views is what matters. If you wish to spread a session over two or more meetings, that's fine.

- You might decide to play all or part of the cassette at the end as well as the beginning. If you decide to use *an extract*, you are advised to use a different copy of the cassette from that used at the beginning – ready at the precise point (finding a specific place can be difficult, especially when others are watching!).

- For some questions you might start with a couple of minutes' silence to make jottings – or by asking members to talk in sub-groups of two or three before sharing with the whole group.

- Decide in advance if you want to distribute (or ask people to bring) paper, pencil, Bibles, hymn books, etc. If possible, ask people *in advance* to read a passage or lead in prayer – so that they can prepare.

- You might wish to read one of the Summaries to start or end a session. These are entitled, 'How Can I Become a Disciple?' (p. 24) and 'What it Means to Be a Christian' (p. 129).

York Courses have produced several audio-tapes which accompany the text of some of the courses in this book. Further details may be obtained from:

York Courses, St Barnabas Vicarage, PO Box 343, York, YO19 5YB (phone 01904-481677 or 654214, fax 01904-481102, email yorkcourses@barn.clara.net)

FIRST COURSE

Some Themes from the Teaching of Jesus

SESSION 1: FORGIVENESS

When I was a young teacher I found myself organising a school sports day. It was hard work. Weeks of planning, much running around on the day itself, and a great deal of diplomacy (Mr Brown did *not* want to spend the afternoon measuring the long-jump pit!).

All went well until after the event, when the deputy head complained that chairs for the spectators were still on the field. Not a word of thanks, not a hint of 'well done', just a complaint about the one area of responsibility which *wasn't* mine.

What should I do? Inform him that Mrs Green was responsible for the chairs? Tell him that he could find someone else to organise Sports Day next year? Well, two things were clear. First, I felt hopping mad. Second, I must forgive the deputy head despite his ungracious behaviour. But what did that mean exactly? Was I obliged to forget the whole thing by the next morning? Should I feel warm thoughts towards him? Must I act like a doormat? Or what?

I've told that trivial story, because the practice of forgiveness for most of us comes in the undramatic circumstances of daily life. Fred's thoughtlessness, Sue's unkindness, Bill's laziness, Mary's unreliability. It was these tiny items of grit in the oyster of daily life that the apostle had in mind when he wrote this most beautiful paragraph:

Therefore, as God's chosen people, holy and dearly loved, clothe yourselves with compassion, kindness, humility,

> gentleness and patience. Bear with each other and forgive
> whatever grievances you may have against one another.
> Forgive as the Lord forgave you. And over all these virtues
> put on love, which binds them all together in perfect unity.
> (Col. 3:12–14)

That passage is beautiful. It is also surprising – even disturbing. For
we might expect Christians to do rather better. Why on earth
should they *need* such teaching?

One definition of love which has stayed with me (from a book
entitled *Psychiatry Reassessed*, of all things) is: 'a thousand acts of
kindness, courtesy and thoughtfulness'. Clearly – and sadly – those
early believers were no better at this than we are. And, like us,
when they were on the receiving end of mediocre and unloving
behaviour, they felt aggrieved.

But why is forgiveness so important, and why did Jesus keep
talking about it? What's wrong with a little private luxury of
resentment? The answer, I guess, is twofold. First, lack of forgiveness always leads to a spiral of bitterness; relationships degenerate
and decay. Second, because if we harbour grudges, they eat away
at us *from the inside*.

World heavyweight champion Ivander Holyfield illustrates this.
He is a devout Christian and he and his team start each training
day with prayer. How did he feel about the man who bit a chunk
from his ear? He forgave him – making the point that if he did not
forgive, Mike Tyson would have inflicted a twofold injury: to his
body *and* deep within his soul. *Bitterness locks us into the past;
forgiveness releases us into the future.* These vital insights are captured
vividly by Steve Chalke on the cassette when he says: 'There is an
old Chinese proverb which says: "Let him who seeks revenge,
remember to dig two graves." '

I've kept all this at a fairly mundane level (I don't include
Holyfield's savaged ear in that description) because – thank God –
the practice of forgiveness stops there for most of us. But some
human beings have a much tougher path to tread. There are people
walking our streets who are scarred by memories of perpetual
bullying, or damaged by abuse throughout childhood. And some

live daily with the knowledge that their son or daughter was tormented and raped before being killed. Perhaps nothing can touch them apart from a tortured man dying on a cross, who said: 'Father, forgive them, for they know not what they do.'

This course is accompanied by an audio-tape with fifteen 5-minute 'programmes' (one for each session) featuring:
- DR DAVID HOPE, Archbishop of York
- PROFESSOR JAMES DUNN of Durham University
- STEVE CHALKE, Baptist minister, founder of the Oasis Trust, and television presenter
- DR PAULINE WEBB, a Methodist and former Head of Religious Broadcasting for the BBC World Service

The cassette can be ordered from: York Courses, St Barnabas Vicarage, PO Box 343, York, YO19 5YB (phone 01904-481677 or 654214, fax 01904-481102) email yorkcourses@barn.clara.net

---

- **DR PAULINE WEBB**   Jesus realised that forgiveness is one of the deepest needs of the human heart. We have all fallen short of the mark – which is what the Bible says sin is. We have all fallen short of what God intends for us and we need to know ourselves forgiven, because it is only through knowing that, that we understand how to forgive other people.
- **STEVE CHALKE**   We think about church as being for the righteous – for those who have got their lives together. What we have not got across is that God is love . . . forgiveness is the most important message that Jesus preached within the theme 'God is love'. Love and forgiveness fit together.
- **DR DAVID HOPE, ARCHBISHOP OF YORK**   If there really has been a big difference of opinion, or you've had a big disagreement, and you really feel pretty wounded and cut up about it and someone says, 'Will you forgive me?', it can actually cost quite a lot to give forgiveness – and even to receive forgiveness. Perhaps that's even harder.

• **PROFESSOR JAMES DUNN**   The death of Jesus is a way
  of saying to us that forgiveness is costly. Forgiveness which does
  not cost you something may not therefore be real forgiveness.
  Because what we are talking about in sin is damage to relationships and individuals. Sin is a kind of cancer. To cut this out is
  a costly thing – painful, sore.

Questions for Discussion
*Note: It is unlikely that you will tackle all the questions in one sitting.
Please select those which suit your situation, or spread each session over
two weeks.*

Suggested reading: Luke 6:37–42.
1   What did forgiveness mean for John Young? Was he obliged
    to forget the whole thing by the next morning? Should he feel
    warm thoughts towards the deputy head? Should he act like a
    doormat? Or what? Does Rosemary Harthill provide a clue
    when she says, 'I'd rather believe in transforming power, than
    clean breaks with the past'?
2   Can you share with other group members your biggest encour-
    agement to practise forgiveness? e.g. an example, a sermon, a
    book . . .
3   Can you share with other group members your biggest struggle
    with forgiveness? *Either*
    (a) in giving it,
    (b) in asking for it – from God or from another person, or
    (c) in receiving it – from God or from another person.
4   'Bitterness locks us into the past; forgiveness releases us into
    the future.' Do you agree?
5   'I can never forgive him/her.'
    (a) Have you ever heard that statement? In what circum-
        stances?
    (b) Have you ever made that statement? In what circum-
        stances?
    (c) How would you respond if you heard someone say that?
6   If someone said, 'My biggest problem is to forgive myself,' or,
    'I find it hard to forgive God,' what would you say to them?

7   Is the teaching of Jesus idealistic but impractical?
    e.g. Turn the other cheek; forgive seventy times seven times.
8   James Jones, Bishop of Liverpool, was asked about the
    Hillsborough football disaster. He spoke about the need to
    forgive but added that when emotional wounds are very deep
    it takes time to develop a spirit of forgiveness – a process which
    cannot be rushed. Do you agree with him?
9   In the Bible our forgiveness appears to depend upon two
    things:
    (a) a willingness to forgive one another
    (b) the death of Jesus – in dying, he ratified a new covenant
         which includes the forgiveness of sins (Matt. 26:28).
    How important in your personal life – and especially in
    combating personal bitterness and anger – is the death of Jesus?
10 A London rector was clubbed unconscious and his daughter
    was raped. He said that he fully forgave his attackers but hoped
    that they would get very stiff prison sentences. Does his attitude
    contain a contradiction?

Close by reading and saying together – slowly and thoughtfully –
the Lord's Prayer.

SESSION 2: JESUS' TEACHING ABOUT GOD

Jesus' teaching about God was very simple. He took an old idea from the Jewish Scriptures and made it central to his message. Think of God as a very good father – and you've got it in one. '. . . your heavenly Father knows that you need these things' (Matt. 6:32).

This was typical of Jesus. He did not set out to be an original teacher. His thought was saturated in the Hebrew Scriptures and he was aware of standing in the flow of a rich tradition. But Jesus *was* original nonetheless. For he drew new connections, and he made fresh emphases. He was aware that tradition had, in many areas, drawn a curtain of dust over the living Word of God. As Jesus blew the dust away, he created a sandstorm.

Question: If you were to select just one Bible word as a title for the first essay in a book called *The Central Message of the New Testament*, what would that word be? Forty years ago the German scholar Joachim Jeremias set himself that task. The word he came up with was . . . *Abba*, the Aramaic word for Father.

Jeremias made two points which were to become famous. First, *Abba* was an intimate, family word for father. It was the expression of a trusting child. 'Dad' or 'Daddy' is the nearest we can get. Second, Jesus was unique among his contemporaries in praying to God in this way (Mark 14:36). The second point has been contested by other scholars (e.g. James Barr), but one thing remains certain – the word *Abba* is Jesus' gift to his disciples. Not just the word, but the close relationship of trust and intimacy which it communicates.

It is not surprising that *Jesus* could address God in this way, for as God's voice at Jesus' baptism reminds us, this is 'my Son, whom I love' (Luke 3:22). But it is surprising that *we* are encouraged – no, *required* – to approach God in that same direct, personal way (e.g. Rom. 8:15; Gal. 4:6; Heb. 4:16).

Familiarity with the New Testament – a good thing in itself, of course – means that we can miss the force of some of its more remarkable features. One such feature is the fact that the apostle Paul could write to Christians in far-away Rome, within thirty years of Jesus' death, and assume that they knew and appreciated an *Aramaic* word. It is as though a Welsh word should become vital for Cockneys!

That word is *Abba* – the gift of Jesus to all believers. It takes us to the heart of our faith. The great and holy God is concerned not only with the large story of the universe. He is concerned with an almost infinite number of small stories too. 'Human story touches human story in the midst of God's story' as the Anglican Primates put it after the 1988 Lambeth Conference. 'Even the hairs on your head are numbered' as Another put it, two thousand years earlier.

But that isn't the end of the story. Jesus' teaching encourages intimacy and trust. But it forbids chumminess. He talks often about the Kingdom – or rule – of God. We are to love God, to trust God – and to *fear* God. For God is GOD. The children in the Narnia tales romp and play with Aslan the lion. But the occasional growl reminds them that he is wild, not tame. They may be princes and princesses, but *he* is KING.

What are the practical implications of all that? For our answer we turn to the quotations from the cassette and to the questions.

- **PROFESSOR JAMES DUNN** The dominant image which Jesus would encourage us to take is the image of God as Father and . . . one thing we can be sure about is that God's mercy will exceed ours and exceed our conception of God's mercy.
- **DR PAULINE WEBB** The Kingdom of God is like having an embassy of another kingdom present in our midst, where the rules of that other kingdom prevail and where we can catch a glimpse of what sort of a kingdom that is. I sometimes think that the Church should be an embassy of the Kingdom of God; it's what the Church is meant to be. It *ought* to show us what the Kingdom of God should be like – what it *would* be like, if we all lived as God wanted us to live.

- **STEVE CHALKE**   God's Kingdom is seen in my life in as far as I am like him. His values are those of love, compassion, justice, mercy, forgiveness. As I display those traits, I am within God's Kingdom, God's will, God's authority. In as far as I don't display those I'm beyond his Kingdom . . . The Church and the Kingdom of God are not necessarily the same thing. Insofar as the local church exhibits God's qualities, it is within the Kingdom. Where it doesn't, it rests outside God's Kingdom.
- **THE ARCHBISHOP OF YORK**   In my own pastoral ministry, when I visited the family of someone who had died a painful death, I sometimes found tremendous anger. My presence there is not to say very much, because in the face of the paradox of a loving God and suffering humanity, we are in the presence of an unfathomable mystery. Silence is, I think, sometimes the only proper response – and to signify God's care by being there. And attempting to soak up that anger which is being expressed – hopefully for that person's inner healing.

(*Note*: *The above quotations are taken from the audio-tape which accompanies this course. See p. 3.*)

Questions for Groups
Suggested reading: Matthew 6:25–34.

1 Raise any points from the cassette or text with which you strongly agree or disagree.
2 Share one concrete example where your own faith in God connected with real life (health, money, relationships, etc., are all grist to this mill).
3 Re-read the quotations from Steve Chalke and Pauline Webb about the Church and the Kingdom of God. What practical steps can you take to bring *your* church more firmly into God's Kingdom?
4 'When I stop praying, coincidences stop happening' (Archbishop William Temple). On the cassette, Steve Chalke saw a

remarkable financial gift as an answer to prayer. Was he right? Can you give other examples of answered prayer – from your own life or others?

5   The New Testament gives some famous examples of God answering prayer with a 'No' (e.g. Luke 22:42; 2 Cor. 12:8,9). On the cassette, Pauline Webb interprets her sister's death as an answer to prayer, on the basis that God knows the whole future. Is that acceptable to you? Or is it a case of 'heads I win; tails I win, too'?

6   *Bible study*: Look up Psalm 7:10–11 and Psalm 95.
    (a) Which five images of God emerge? (You might wish to add other images – from memory or by scanning the Psalms.)
    (b) What do these – together with the term '*Abba*, Father' – tell us about the God whom we worship?
    (c) Do these images of God give you confidence for living?

7   Some believers want to balance the Father image of God with the Mother image. Others see this as a 'politically correct' attack on traditional faith. Where do you stand on this? (You might wish to replay the relevant section of the cassette.)

8   Each share one story of suffering known to you. Does it shake or strengthen your faith in God as *Abba*, Father?

9   *Is* there a difference between coming to God with confidence (as we should: see Hebrews 4:16) and 'chumminess'? If so, what practical steps – in worship and in daily life – can we take to grow in confidence and diminish in chumminess?

10 (a) 'To argue that God exists is to deny him' (Paul Tillich).
    (b) 'He who believes without having any reason for believing may be in love with his own fancies' (John Locke).
    Which side do you come down on, and why?

You might close by reading one of the Summaries on pp. 24 and 129 (using several voices).

SESSION 3: JESUS' TEACHING ON MONEY

'The last corner of a person to be converted is likely to be the pocket.' I've pondered that saying over the years and come to the conclusion that – in my case anyway – it isn't true. My pocket was converted early on. When I was at theological college, there was an appeal on behalf of a Korean orphanage. Not one-tenth of my worldly wealth went into that collection, but nearer nine-tenths. I doubt that I'd do that today. Partly because I have more money; partly because I feel a stronger urge to hang on to it.

Surely that's reasonable? After all, I am moving at the speed of light towards retirement. It is sensible to save for my old age. It is necessary to save for my wife's final years. And I have an elderly mother, two married children and three grandchildren. I must prepare for the proverbial rainy day.

Yes, but . . . For into the middle of all those perfectly reasonable thoughts about not becoming a burden on my family and deserving a few holidays in the sun, come the words of Jesus: 'Sell your possessions and give to the poor.' It's not simply a sentence; it's a torpedo. No wonder the rich young ruler turned on his heel and walked away.

Fortunately, there might be a way out of the tight corner. For quite often Jesus said things which he didn't really mean:

- Hate your father and your mother.
- Leave the dead to bury the dead.
- Cut off your hand if it's leading you into sin.

Anyone who takes those statements literally doesn't understand how language works.

Perhaps Jesus' talk about money falls into the same category? After all, he didn't seem to practise what he preached in this department. He may not have been wealthy, but his group of wandering disciples shared a common purse. And they depended on a small group of women who had funds (Luke 8:3). Members of the early Church owned property. They gathered in homes, and they had the wherewithal to buy bread to break and wine to pour.

In this way I convinced myself that I'd found a solution to my uneasy conscience. My bank account didn't need radical surgery after all. Then I received a letter from Peru. A seventy-year-old pastor (whom I've met) wants to retire. But with little or no state support, and an impoverished church, how can he do so? So I'm back at the beginning again. Literally at the beginning – in Genesis 3 – with the sharp question to which we all know the answer. 'Am I my brother's keeper?' No, I can't solve the problems of world poverty. But I might be able to help solve a pressing practical problem for one or two families.

There's even more to it than that, of course. When Jesus challenges us not to grow our nest egg too big, he's as concerned for us as for the world's poor. 'Where your treasure is, there your heart will be also' (Luke 12:34). If we gain our security from our savings, we are less likely to seek our security from our Lord. It seems that the life of faith can't easily flourish in the soil of abundance, as the parable of the sower makes clear.

> The seed that fell among thorns stands for those who hear, but as they go on their way they are choked by life's worries, riches and pleasures, and they do not mature. But the seed on good soil stands for those with a noble and good heart who hear the word, retain it, and by persevering produce a crop. (Luke 8:14, 15)

As Jesus also said, 'Those who have ears to hear, let them hear.'

- **DR PAULINE WEBB** Selling your possessions means, in a way, giving up your power. That's what money's all about, isn't it? You've got power to choose what you do with it; you've

got power over other people. I think Jesus was saying to the
rich young ruler – you need to give up your power as Jesus
himself had done, and learn to live in his way. I think he's
saying the same thing to us.

- **STEVE CHALKE**   Tithing is very good news for very rich
  people. It's a great comfort to know that all I have to do is give
  away 10 per cent and I can keep 90 per cent for me. What the
  Bible teaches is tithing *plus*. In the Old Testament they brought
  their tithes *and* their offerings. You bring the one-tenth as a
  matter of course – as a duty – and your offering is what you give
  over and above that. Tithing is the *beginning* place, not the
  ending place.

- **ARCHBISHOP DAVID HOPE**   Money, along with
  everything else, is a gift from God – and we don't always
  recognise that very well. Maybe the modern Church needs to
  hear again something of the clarity, simplicity and radical nature
  of this particular call of Jesus. In other words, perhaps what
  we're looking for is a new asceticism in the life of the Church
  . . . one very significant fact is that per capita giving is far more
  substantial in some of our urban, poorer, deprived areas than it
  is in many other parishes.

- **PROFESSOR JAMES DUNN**   Yes, the teaching of Jesus
  on wealth is bad news for rich people. 'How hard shall it be for
  a rich man to enter the Kingdom of Heaven,' said Jesus. The
  danger always for the rich – and that includes the relatively rich
  – is that they trust too much in their wealth and build their lives
  on their wealth. They 'lay up treasure on earth', and if you lay
  up treasure on earth, it's hard also to lay up treasure in heaven
  . . . It's a question for the individual – how much are you
  committed to this cause and is your commitment adequately
  expressed in what you give?

Questions for Groups
Suggested reading: Luke 12:27–34.

1   Note any points from the cassette or notes with which you
    strongly agree or disagree.
2   Re-read Steve Chalke's point about tithing *plus*. Is he being

realistic or hopelessly impractical? At the same time, you might consider the assertion that, 'It's not a question of how much of my money I give to God, but how much of God's money I keep for myself.'

3   A church treasurer was raising money to employ a much-needed part-time youth worker. He said, 'The good news is that we have all the money we need. The bad news is that it's in your pockets.' Comments, please!

4   What do you make of the Archbishop's assertion about giving by people in poorer churches? Is this true in your experience?

5   Re-read the quotations from Pauline Webb and James Dunn. Do you feel the force of what they say? What might this mean for your church, for your discussion group – and for you as an individual?

6   On the cassette James Dunn says: 'If you put your trust in your wealth then you're in grave danger, whether you're relatively poor or relatively rich. But it is quite possible for people to be very rich and to use their riches for good purposes.' Can his comments be squared with the teaching of Jesus?

7   Look up 1 Corinthians 16:2 where St Paul urges believers to be methodical in their giving. Is giving for you a matter of instinct – or do you sit down and work out the figures from time to time? Are you happy with your approach, or do you feel that you should review it?

8   Some people feel that the Church is always asking for money. If so, it gets in the way of the Gospel of God's free grace. Yet the Church must pay its bills. Do you feel the force of this tension, and how may it be resolved?

9   What do you understand by the Archbishop's statement, 'Perhaps what we're looking for is a new asceticism in the life of the Church'? Do you agree with him? What might that mean in practical terms?

10 Is your church setting a good example to its members – e.g. does it give a set proportion of its income to world mission agencies? Should it, in your view? Is it legitimate to say that local needs are too pressing – or is that another way of saying

that other (even more urgent) needs are real but invisible and I am *not* my brother's keeper?

Read 2 Corinthians 8:8–15 and say the Grace together.

SESSION 4: JESUS ON HEAVEN AND HELL

Charles Darwin gradually lost his Christian faith, not as a result of his scientific investigations but for personal and emotional reasons. First, there was the death of his daughter. Then there was the unpalatable doctrine of hell which, he felt, reduced God to a monster. Others have felt the force of this viewpoint: Bertrand Russell, for example.

Nowadays the doctrine of hell is less of a problem, for it is less prominent in the Church's teaching. We prefer to talk about God's unconditional love. But is this true to the New Testament – and especially to the teaching of Jesus? In one sense, yes. God's love *is* unconditional, in that it is for everyone, regardless of moral rectitude. 'The Son of Man came to seek and to save that which was lost' (Luke 19:10). But there is *one* condition. His forgiveness has to be received. The gift must be unwrapped and accepted. We do this by coming with empty hands and open hearts. An open heart involves a measure of faith (tiny as a mustard seed will do) and repentance.

The common view, that Jesus taught sweetness and light and then that nasty St Paul came and muddied the waters, simply doesn't hold up to scrutiny. Our hope that universalism may be true and that all will be saved – and which Christian with a tender heart does not wish for that – is encouraged only by occasional passages in Paul's letters (1 Cor. 15:22, for example). It is Jesus who talks about fire, worms and outer darkness 'where there will be weeping and gnashing of teeth' (Matt. 8:12).

We know that to take Jesus' teaching literally is sometimes to court disaster. If we always do so, we shall end up hating our parents, severing our limbs and keeping corpses in our homes (Matt. 8:22). So a knowledge of the way in which Jesus used language may reduce the sting of his teaching about hell (*Gehenna* in Greek). But it does not remove it altogether. What remains is a strong sense that eternal issues are being settled *right now in our everyday lives* – by the decisions we make, by the money we spend, by the kind of relationships we establish and develop.

C.S. Lewis put this with great force in his famous Oxford sermon 'The Weight of Glory'.

> It is a serious thing . . . to remember that the dullest and most uninteresting person you talk to may one day be a creature which, if you saw it now, you would be strongly tempted to worship, or else a horror and a corruption which you now meet, if at all, only in a nightmare. All day long we are, in some degree, helping each other to one or other of these destinations. It is in the light of these overwhelming possibilities . . . that we should conduct all our dealings with one another, all friendships, all loves, all play, all politics. There are no *ordinary* people.

W.H. Auden made a related point with equal force:

> All sin tends to be addictive, and the terminal point of addiction is damnation. Since God has given us the freedom either to accept his love and obey the laws of our created nature, or to reject it and defy them, he cannot prevent us from going to hell and staying there if that is what we insist upon.

There *is* a heaven to be gained and a hell to be shunned. And our preparedness for one or the other begins right here and right now. Over the years we become the kind of person who delights to acknowledge Jesus as 'the Lamb upon the throne'. Or we insist on enthroning ourselves at the centre of our own personal universe.

In the end, only four words will be spoken: 'Your will be done.' Spoken by God to us, they assume an awful finality. But if we say those words to God, the gates of Glory will be flung open. Once inside, Jesus assures us that we shall find ourselves in the middle of a swinging party, where everyone is having a wonderful time. Except that time won't exist, of course.

- **PAULINE WEBB**   Hell must be to be cut off altogether from God, and that sometimes begins in this life. Heaven is knowing the love of God, and that begins in this life as well. And I suppose beyond this life it means that it continues and this life isn't all there is.
- **STEVE CHALKE**   Before I became a Christian I was petrified of death – paranoid about the whole thing. I used to lie in bed sometimes and imagine being dead – absolutely terrified. I can say over the years that I've been a Christian, that fear of death has gone. I know, because I trust Christ, there is life beyond death. There is heaven – so I'm not scared of being dead . . . the process of dying is a different matter. You are talking to a man who is scared of going to the dentist!
- **DAVID HOPE**   I take very seriously the teaching of Jesus about heaven and hell. They are states which we already begin to experience. I do need to keep before me the fact that there is a judgement. You think, 'Sinful person that I am' – and yet God is prepared to forgive me. It's an insight into the wonderful and amazing grace of God.
- **JAMES DUNN**   We should envisage the possibility that we lock ourselves into attitudes which become set and definitive for us. I think Jesus has this in mind when he talks about the unforgivable sin. This is not any particular action which you may regret. It refers to the fact that we may live a life which we should regret and don't regret. And the person who lives an unregretted life that should be regretted, is in this kind of plight which is depicted by hell.

Questions for Groups
Suggested reading: Matthew 18:1–9.
1   Note any points in the text or on the cassette with which you strongly agree or disagree.
2   Each of our contributors takes heaven and hell very seriously.
   (a) Do you believe in hell? If so, how do you envisage it?
   (b) Do you believe in heaven? If so, how do you envisage it?
3   Some Christians are quite certain that they will go to heaven.

Others find this boastful and proud. What do you feel about this? (Look up Isaiah 1:18, 1 John 1:8–9, and perhaps read verses 3 and 4 of 'There is a green hill . . .')

4   Steve Chalke is afraid of dying but not afraid of death. Does he speak for you? Share your fears, worries and hopes with other group members, including any experience with dying people.

5   James Dunn said, 'The symbolism of judgement is very important . . . It is important that we should live our lives conscious of our responsibility to a higher authority.' Do you feel the force of this? Does it affect your life in a practical way?

6   Read and discuss the following paragraph by Gillian Evans:
    We should not think of heaven as being in one place for endless 'time'. We should be envisaging a freedom from the confinement of time and space which will make it possible for us to be with all our friends at once and individually, to be enjoying an infinite variety of things as we choose . . . It is something new, a new quality of life.

7   The Church in previous centuries is often criticised for placing too much emphasis on hell and damnation. The modern Church is sometimes criticised for placing too little emphasis on God's judgement and wrath.
    (a) Do you think these criticisms are valid?
    (b) When did you last hear a sermon on heaven?
    (c) When did you last hear a sermon on hell?

8   Do you (like C.S. Lewis) view other people as infinite beings of infinite significance – destined for heaven or hell? If so, what are the practical implications?

9   Read the Parable of the Sheep and the Goats (Matt. 25:31–46).
    (a) Can you find a word to sum up your response? e.g. surprise, unease, challenge, inspiration, terror?
    (b) Does the parable point to the need for concerted political action – lobbying for fair trade and the remission of third world debt, for example?

10 *Bible study*: When teaching about his second coming in great glory, Jesus told his disciples: 'Be on guard! Be alert!' (Mark 13:33). When pondering the same theme, Paul urged his

readers to 'wake up' (Rom. 13:11; Eph. 5:14; 1 Thess. 5:6). What might these sharp phrases mean for us in practical terms?

SESSION 5: ON BEING HUMAN

Our view of human nature, like our view of God, has immense practical implications. In particular, it influences the way we rear and educate our children. Assume that children have a perverse will that must be broken, and child-rearing becomes repressive and cruel. Take the view that children are full of natural goodness, and they may grow up without healthy constraints and necessary discipline. History illustrates the practical importance of theories of human nature.

Jesus was ruggedly realistic and utterly unsentimental. 'You, then, being evil . . .' That, of course, is only the starting point. We rejoice that Jesus was in the business of *changing* human nature. 'Now Zaccheus was a very little man' goes the children's chorus. It ends charmingly with the words, 'For I'm coming to your house for tea'. It is more likely that they drank wine, but no matter. What does matter is that, ever since, Jesus has been visiting people's homes for tea and transformation.

Malcolm Worsley is a good example. On the day of yet another release from prison, a prison officer remarked, 'You'll be back, Worsley.' That officer was right. Malcolm did return, but as a member of staff! For Malcolm had been converted to Christ. He trained as a probation officer, and worked with people who were dependent on drugs. In July 1996, Malcolm was ordained as a minister in the Church of England.

Malcolm Worsley's experience gives deep insights into what it means to be a human being. The degradation that spoils our lives. And the remarkable possibilities for grace and glory which are always in front of us. Paul summed this up in a striking sentence: 'If anyone is in Christ, he is a new creation' (2 Cor. 5:17).

To be human beings is our high calling. Are there other equally high callings in other parts of the universe? Perhaps there are; perhaps we shall never know. But this we do know – that 'God so loved the world that he gave his one and only Son' (John 3:16). His Son calls us to follow him and he calls us to do this *together*. The philosopher John MacMurray wrote a book entitled *Persons in Relation* in which he asserted that the basic unit for human beings was not one person, but two. Friendship, support and mutual encouragement are central to the Bible and were key ingredients in the spread of the Gospel.

Nothing signals the dignity of what it means to be a human being more clearly than the incarnation, crucifixion and ascension of Jesus. He was born among us, became one of us and – according to the New Testament – shared our lives in every respect apart from sin. And he died among us and for us.

At his ascension Jesus did not lay aside his humanity. He took it back with him into heaven. It is not an angel who is seated at the Father's right hand – it is *'the man* Christ Jesus' (1 Tim. 2:5).

But Jesus is not locked away from us. Every day he comes to us by his Spirit. To a world beset by problems he comes as guide. In a world where many are lonely, he comes as friend. To a world which often seems to lack meaning, he brings understanding. For a world tempted to despair, he provides the ground of hope. Over a world where dying is the single certainty, he sits enthroned as the conqueror of death.

The words of Jesus, as recorded by St John, have been tested and proved in the lives of countless thousands of men and women: 'I am the light of the world. Whoever follows me will never walk in darkness but will have the light of life' (John 8:12).

- **PAULINE WEBB** Jesus was realistic about human nature but what I think he would not agree with is, 'You can't change human nature'. I think he would say you can, because he saw that happen – he *made* it happen with people like Zaccheus. He was pessimistic about human nature, but optimistic about what the grace of God can do with it.
- **STEVE CHALKE** Jesus was very realistic about human nature. The whole Bible is realistic about human nature, which is why the Bible is not a self-help book. It is a God-help book. It doesn't just tell us how to live – although it has much to say

about that. It tells us that at the heart of life what we most need is forgiveness and what we need after that is empowerment. At the heart of the Bible is this message: that God forgives us, then fills us with his Spirit to equip us to be the kind of people that God longs for us to be.

- **DAVID HOPE** It does seem to me that there is a very effective model for us in the New Testament – for family life and the nature of human relations. For example, the context in which Jesus is born – the Holy Family of Joseph, Mary and Jesus – and the nature of his relationships with his friends. He calls into their homes – there is a hospitality and reciprocity of life and living. The New Testament sets before us the ideals and standards, while being realistic about where people actually find themselves. The whole point is that Jesus is there with us and alongside those whose lives have, in various ways, broken down, come unstuck, are disordered . . .

- **JAMES DUNN** Pride is a way of speaking about that funda-mental sin where a human creature tries to be as God – that is, to have control over his own destiny and over the destiny of others. And that is the beginning of all calamity.

Questions for Groups
Suggested readings: Mark 7:14–23 and Luke 11:9–13.

1 Pick out any points on the cassette or in the text with which you strongly agree or disagree.

2 Social psychologist Michael Argyle (who is not a Christian) claims research evidence to show that people with a strong belief in God are happier. They also live longer. Why might this be?

3 'You can't change human nature.' How would you respond to this assertion?

4 David Hope stresses Jesus' friendships and the importance of hospitality for his ministry. James Dunn fears that we may be losing this in the modern Church. Score your own church for hospitality/friendship on a scale of 1–10. How can you improve your score?

5 'Send us out in the power of your Spirit.' Steve Chalke and

David Hope insist that all true theology – like all true worship – has practical implications. We could go further – arguing that we need theology (literally, words about God) to make sense of being human. What are your views on this?

6   C.S. Lewis argued that there may be intelligent beings on other planets who (a) need no act of redemption *or* (b) have been saved by Christ in a way appropriate for them. What do you make of this?

7   Do you *love* God, *trust* God and *fear* God? What does this mean in practical terms and how can you improve in these areas?

8   Divide your group into two.
    Sub-Group A role-plays the view of some atheists that Christians are whimps – leaning on God for support, instead of standing on their own two feet.
    Sub-Group B represents the Christian view that we all depend on God for life itself and that faith can lead to heroism and sacrifice. Let battle commence!

9   Do the implications of the incarnation, crucifixion and ascension, outlined in the article, excite you? If so, why? If not, why not?

10 Faith in God must involve adventure and risk, which are key ingredients in being a fulfilled human being. Score yourself on a 1–10 scale (1 = too cautious in life; 10 = too wild!). Ask other group members to help you improve your score.

Close by reading John 10:7–10 and saying the Lord's Prayer.

FIRST SUMMARY:

How Can I Become a Disciple?

In support of a city-wide ecumenical mission, Father Cyril – a much loved Benedictine monk – cycled 2,000 miles in twenty-one days. He pedalled from York to Land's End, from Land's End to John O'Groats, then back to York again. This would be a tremendous feat for a young man; at sixty-two it was extraordinary.

The first day was easy. The sun shone, his bike was trouble-free, his legs were strong. Of course, Cyril knew that some of the next twenty-one days would not be like that. He had started a great adventure and there was no way of knowing what lay ahead.

Becoming a disciple of Jesus is like that. Think of Peter. One sunny morning Jesus said, 'Follow me,' and he did just that. Had Peter realised that ahead of him lay conflict as well as fellowship and crucifixion as well as fame, he might have acted differently.

So with us. Jesus promises 'life in all its fullness' (John 10:10, GNB). He does not promise roses all the way. Become a Christian and you might be in for *anything*. But getting started is easy: it involves careful reflection and a simple but sincere prayer.

- *Reflect on your life*
  Reflect on your relationships, on your goals, on your strengths and weaknesses, on your needs, on your moral standards. If you feel satisfied on all these fronts then you need go no further, for the Christian faith has little to offer you at present. But if you feel a sense of what things *might* be – given a new start and help from God and other people – then you have already taken the first step.
- *Reflect on Jesus*
  Reflect on the impact of this amazing man who chopped history in half. Then reflect on the significance of his death. The Bible claims that in dying on the cross Jesus did something incredibly

important for all of us. 'He died that we might be forgiven', as the old hymn puts it.

This is why baptism and Holy Communion are so important. They link us *now* with his death *then*. Holy Communion takes us back to the night when Jesus ate the Last Supper with his friends. It was the night before he died – and four days before he rose again.

- *Open your life to him*

Jesus was too good and too great to be held by death. God raised him from the grave. He is alive today, and by his Spirit (the Holy Spirit) he is active in our world and in our lives. This is the Christian claim, and this is the Christian challenge, too.

Because Jesus is alive, he wants to share your life – every aspect of it. If you want this too, then simply invite him into your life. Millions of people have done this and they testify to two things.

Jesus brings them great comfort and strength. He comes to us in gentleness and love, offering forgiveness for sins and healing for hurts.

Jesus also disturbs and makes them feel uncomfortable. He comes into our lives as a restless guest. He wants to raise our horizons, to make us more aware of other people and their needs, to tame wild people and make tame people more wild. In short, he calls us to the adventure of living by faith.

- *Speak to him in prayer*

You may wish to make up a prayer of your own or use the prayer set out below:

Lord Jesus Christ, I want to follow you. Help me to know that you are with me day by day. Please forgive me for all the wrong things which I do and think and say, and give me strength to do better. Help me to make you the Lord of my life – and help me to show this by loving and serving other people. Amen.

Where Now?

- *You are invited to sign* and date the following simple but momentous statement as a concrete reminder that you are a disciple of Jesus.

  On this date . . . . after careful consideration
  I invited the risen Lord to share my life.

  Signed . . . .

- *Link up with a local church*. Jesus does not want solitary disciples. He wants a family of believers who can give and receive support and encouragement. If you haven't been baptised then this great joy is in store. Or perhaps you will find a church which has other ways of welcoming newcomers (the Right Hand of Fellowship, confirmation, signing the Roll of Church Membership, etc.).

Note: The second Summary may be found on p. 129.

SECOND COURSE

Great Events – Deep Meanings

SESSION 1: CHRISTMAS

Note: This course is based on some of the great festivals and holy days in the Christian year. It was originally written for Lent but may be used at any time. Considering the meaning of Christmas in June, or Pentecost in January, might well throw new light on these great seasons!

To get us into the spirit of Christmas, let's begin with a cracker-style question. Which single word links *The X Files*, *Independence Day*, recent scientific research and John Betjeman? The answer is . . . ***wistfulness***.

A survey of television and film viewing can reveal a great deal about the psychology of a nation. Popular programmes like *The X Files* and films like *Independence Day* raise a fascinating question. 'Is there anyone out there? Or are we inhabitants of planet Earth, alone in the universe?' Recently this was given impetus by a group of scientists who claimed to have found primitive life on Mars. Inevitably, their views were disputed by other scientists.

In a rather different way, Christmas raises the same question – and it gives a powerful answer. In J.B. Phillips' memorable phrase, we are a 'visited' planet. For, according to the Christmas story, the baby lying in a manger – tiny and vulnerable – is *Emmanuel*, 'God with us'. *Here* is the guarantee that we are not on our own. *Here* is the assurance that we can find love at the heart and centre of our world.

This is why Christmas causes wistfulness in so many people. They *want* to believe the story, not just for its beauty and power, but because they realise that so much hangs upon it.

Do we live in a cold, uncaring, unfeeling world which grinds

relentlessly on, reducing us all to rubble and dust in the end? Do
we bumble around for seventy or eighty years only to fall off the
edge into empty nothingness? Or are we here through the will and
design of a loving God, who has created us to love him and one
another through all eternity?

These deep, Hamlet-style questions hang around at the edge of
our minds. Most of the time we are too busy with our daily lives
to let them take centre stage. There's work to be done, there are
holidays to be planned, children to get to school, dogs to walk.
Then something happens. A friend dies or we fall ill or we celebrate
yet another birthday with an '0' at the end – and the questions
press in. Many people – including some outside the churches –
instinctively realise that the answers to the deepest questions are
linked with the Baby lying in a manger. With John Betjeman we
ask:

> And is it true? And is it true?
> This most tremendous tale of all . . .
> That God was Man in Palestine
> And lives today in Bread and Wine.

'And is it true?' Our contributors address this central question and
come up with a unanimous '*Yes*'.

Christmas can be sentimentalised to the point where it has no
connection with real life. In fact, it's those who put most weight
on the truth of that story who often seem to be able to handle the
toughest problems. This is certainly true of our participants. As we
hear on the cassette, each of them has had his or her faith tested in
the fires of life, sometimes publicly and famously. We think of
Gordon Wilson, who forgave his daughter's murderers. And Fiona
Castle, who replied to more than 6,000 letters when Roy's lung
cancer was diagnosed, and who found herself in the nation's
headlines when he died.

Gordon and Fiona both see the Baby in a manger as *the* answer
to the great riddles of life and death. *He* is the focus and the
guarantee of the love of God – and of God's involvement in our
world.

Saviour

'You shall call his name Jesus,' said the angel to Joseph, 'For he will save his people from their sins' (Matt. 1:21). Calling Jesus 'Saviour' can sound very 'religious'. In fact it has immense practical significance. The reassurance which we find in the story must be matched by its challenge.

Jesus came to save us. The sins which mark our lives may not be very spectacular – but they are very nasty. Gossip, greed, jealousy, lust, laziness, irritability, unkindness, an ungenerous spirit, thoughtlessness, pettiness, selfishness. These are the attitudes which blight our lives, spoil our relationships and hurt the people with whom we live and work.

We recall – perhaps with embarrassment and shame – the Christian claim that by his example and teaching, and through the forgiveness and new life which he offers, Jesus is able to save us. Critics of Christianity sometimes observe that they could believe in the Saviour more readily, if they found more evidence of salvation in the lives of his followers.

Over to you – and over to me.

An audio-tape accompanies this course with six 15-minute 'programmes' (one for each session). The following quotations are taken from this. The tape features:

- FIONA CASTLE, well-known author, and widow of Roy the entertainer
- REVD BRIAN HOARE, a past president of the Methodist Conference
- DR DAVID HOPE, Archbishop of York
- BISHOP DAVID KONSTANT, Roman Catholic Bishop of Leeds
- PROFESSOR JOHN POLKINGHORNE FRS, Anglican priest and former Professor of Mathematical Physics at Cambridge University
- DAME CICELY SAUNDERS, founder of the international hospice movement

- GORDON WILSON, who became famous for his forgiveness of those who killed his daughter by planting a bomb at a Remembrance Day service in Enniskillen

The audio cassette can be ordered from York Courses. (See p. x for details.)

- **REVD BRIAN HOARE**   Although I confess I love the carols and cards and family reunions, it's tempting to get cynical about Christmas. All that glitter and noisy commercialism seems so far removed from the dirty stable and the stillness of the night when Jesus was born. Yet when I think about it more deeply, Christmas is precisely about God getting involved in the real world – with all its bustle and busyness, its selfishness and superficiality. One of the carol services I remember most vividly was held in a factory canteen in Stoke-on-Trent, in the middle of the working day. Christmas is God making himself at home among us! So one of my favourite titles for Jesus is Emmanuel, 'God with us' in every situation, always and everywhere.
- **DAVID KONSTANT**   The Virgin Birth shows the utter poverty of Mary – that she was called from nothing to be the Mother of God . . . The first symbol, if you like, the first spiritual reality, is mankind's poverty in the presence of God and that everything is a gift.

  I regard the Virgin Birth as a fact. If God is very close to us, then I have no difficulty in accepting that there are occasions when his touch on the world is more direct than is normally the case; more specific.
- **DAVID HOPE**   The real struggle is how to announce the birth of the Saviour in the midst of our culture . . . That's the struggle in every age. How do you speak the truth of the Christian religion to the culture or in the culture?

  The whole point about the incarnation of the Son of God is the fact that God in Jesus Christ has entered into our very deepest human experience of life. There God actually has been – is with us. The Word is made flesh and dwells among us. Emmanuel God – the eternal, everlasting God – is with us, alongside us, for ever and always . . . and that is an immense statement.

- **PROFESSOR JOHN POLKINGHORNE** The Baby in the manger – what does that tell us about God? It tells us that God is prepared to take risks, to be vulnerable, to accept all the dangers of human life. It's the beginning of this exciting Christian idea of God making himself known, in the plainest possible way.

  Christmas is about powerful stories, but about powerful stories which are also true – which have actually happened. If God wants to do a new thing – like becoming a man in Jesus Christ – then nothing that science can tell us about the regularity of the world rules out that possibility.

  It's an astonishingly exciting idea – that God, who is so difficult to think about, has acted to make himself known, by living the life of a man in Jesus Christ. In other words, making himself known in the plainest possible terms. The very miracle of God with us as a small child.

- **FIONA CASTLE** chose as her favourite Christmas carol, 'In the bleak midwinter'. She chose it mainly for the lovely final verse, with its challenge to devotion and commitment.

> What can I give Him,
> Poor as I am?
> If I were a shepherd,
> I would bring a lamb;
> If I were a wise man,
> I would do my part;
> Yet what I can I give Him
> Give my heart.
>
> (Christina Rossetti)

- **DAME CICELY SAUNDERS** Christmas shows the vulnerability of God illustrated in probably the only way it could really reach us. I think it is almost bewilderingly humble.

Christmas Quiz

1   The first Christmas card was produced in
    (a) France 1793? (b) England 1843? (c) Germany 1851?
2   The wise men appear in which Gospel(s)?
    (a) Matthew (b) Mark (c) Luke (d) John
3   The Christmas tree was taken
    (a) to Britain from Germany? (b) to Germany from Britain?
4   Why is mistletoe a 'kissing plant'?
5   What is the relationship between 'Lady Day' and Christmas
    Day?
6   Which Christian festival properly features the wise men?
    (a) Christmas (b) Michaelmas (c) Epiphany (d) Pentecost
7   The Armenian Church celebrates Christmas on
    (a) 6 January? (b) 25 December? (c) 25 June?
8   Jesus was born in the year 0 BC/0 AD True or false?
9   The shepherds appear in which Gospel(s)?
10 Which Gospel(s) has/have no nativity narrative?

1).

10 Mark and John (but St John has the great 'Prologue' in Chapter

9   St Luke.
    miracle!).
8   False: around 6 BC (due to a minor miscalculation, not a major
7   6 January.
6   Epiphany.
5   Lady Day is 25 March, i.e. nine months before Christmas Day.
4   In the Middle Ages it was regarded as a fertility plant.
    to Germany.
    England – and the English missionary St Boniface (680–754) –
3   Both: Queen Victoria's Prince Albert – from Germany to
2   St Matthew.
1   In England in 1843.

Answers to Christmas Quiz

Questions for Groups

Notes to Leaders
1 *I suggest you distribute and tackle the* **Christmas Quiz** *before listening to the cassette – to encourage interaction. Follow this with part one of the cassette and selected questions.*
2 *Before the group listens to the cassette, the leader might give out paper and pens and remind members about Question 3.*
3 *You might have carol sheets or hymn books available for Question 1.*
4 *It is not necessary to tackle all questions. What matters is a lively exchange of views.*
5 *The group might wish to listen to the cassette at the end, as well as the beginning.*

1 What is your favourite Christmas carol, and why?
2 Describe a memorable Christmas or a moment when the 'magic' of Christmas sparked for you.
3 Are there any points from the cassette with which you strongly agree or disagree?
4 A Buddhist visitor asks you to explain the true meaning of Christmas. What would you say? (People might share in pairs before pooling views in the group. After doing this you might listen again to short summaries by the Archbishop of York, Bishop of Leeds and Professor John Polkinghorne at the beginning of the unit on Christmas.)
5 What do you and your church do to make known the good news of Christmas in the midst of so much busyness and commercialism? Do you have ideas on how you could do this more effectively?
6 How do you as an individual (if you do) make sure that you make room for Christ at Christmas? Or do the pressures of family and friends make this seem impossible? (If 'yes' – is this *really* the case?!)
7 Some people have problems with details like angels, the heavenly choir and the guiding star. Do you? Did you find John Polkinghorne's point about symbolism helpful?
8 Did you welcome or object to Bishop David Jenkins'

controversial teaching about the Virgin Birth? Are you happy with Bishop David Konstant's response to those views on the cassette?

Closing Act of Devotion

One member reads Matthew 1:18–23 or John 1:1–14.
Another member prays, perhaps using the following collect:

All praise to you, Almighty God and heavenly king,
who sent your Son into the world
to take our nature upon him
and to be born of a pure virgin.
Grant that, as we are born again in him,
so he may continually dwell in us
and reign on earth as he reigns in heaven
with you and the Holy Spirit,
now and for ever. Amen.

SESSION 2: ASH WEDNESDAY

Christianity is a joyful faith. And, taken overall, the New Testament is a joyful book as it announces 'glad tidings of great joy' (Luke 2:10). This mood was captured by William Tyndale (c. 1494–1536) who worked so hard – and ultimately gave his life – to give our nation a Bible in its own tongue.

> Euangelio (that we cal gospel) is a greke worde, and signyfyth good, mery, glad and joyfull tydings, that maketh a mannes hert glad, and maketh hym syngge, daunce and leepe for joye.

But Christianity is a faith for all seasons, and the Bible speaks to all our moods and all our needs. So while we are encouraged to 'rejoice in the Lord always' (Phil. 4:4), we are also required to confess and repent of our sins. In his letter, James even bids us to weep (Jas. 4:9). Tears are an appropriate response as we reflect on the state of our world, the divisions within Christ's Church and the poverty of our personal spiritual lives.

To help us get the balance of 'moods of faith' right, the church calendar has occasional penitential seasons. After the preparation of Shrove Tuesday, Lent begins on Ash Wednesday – that solemn day which reminds us so powerfully of two unpopular but important truths:

- Our sinfulness
- Our mortality

Surprisingly, Bishop David Konstant speaks of this season as a time of joy. Joy, because we set our sinfulness within the context of the grace and forgiveness of God. Joy, because we contemplate our mortality in the knowledge that by his resurrection, Jesus Christ has flung wide open the gates of Glory. It is vitally important to retain this perspective, for without it Lent can be a spiritual minefield – as the history of the Church makes clear. I can think of at least four dangers.

1 *The danger of spiritual pride* Those who find self-discipline easy might be inclined to feel a sense of spiritual superiority. To guard against this, the Parable of the Pharisee and the Tax-collector (Luke 18:9–14) is often read on Ash Wednesday.

2 *The danger of despair* On the cassette, the Archbishop of York bravely admits to some of his Lenten failures – occasions when he set himself an Olympic schedule, only to find that he ran out of steam.

3 *The danger of hypocrisy* Lent has fluctuated in length – and in severity – throughout the Christian centuries. In the first three centuries it was no more than two or three days. As Lent grew in length, so the rules of fasting became very strict, with only one meal each day, and that not until the evening. As meat, fish, eggs and milk products were usually forbidden, woe betide those who did not like parsnip soup! But fasting was gradually relaxed and ingenious ways of skirting the rules were devised. For example, someone asked the question, 'When does evening begin?' The clear answer was, 'After the evening office of Vespers'. So Vespers was brought forward to before midday! As we smile, we might also examine our own hearts for more modern deceits.

4 *The danger of distorting the Gospel* Salvation is a gift from God and our discipleship is *in response* to God's love, *not* a way of earning it. 'We love because he first loved us' (1 John 4:19). Yet some Lenten hymns give the impression that Lent is a kind of 'do-it-yourself salvation kit':

> Make, Lord, this Lenten discipline
> An expiation for our sin

wrote Bishop W.H. Frere. But he was wrong. For there is only one expiation for our sins – and that is Jesus' death on the cross.

Some Christian traditions give greater prominence to Lent than others. When I asked Gordon Wilson how he kept Lent, he gave a short and honest reply: 'I don't!' But the majority of believers find Lent to be an important element in the rhythm of the Christian year. They find it helpful to have a period of six weeks when they pay greater attention to prayer, penitence, study, self-discipline and the needs of a hungry world. They draw strength to struggle afresh with their own personal demons. They reconsider their involvement in the fight against injustice. And they welcome an opportunity to explore the meaning and significance of their faith, through reading and discussion.

But essentially Lent should be viewed as a preparation. It has no life of its own. It is a time when we watch and pray with our Lord and prepare ourselves to declare with joy, in fellowship with the Church world-wide on Easter Day:

> Alleluia! Christ is risen
> He is risen indeed. Alleluia!

On Discipline

- **DAVID HOPE, ARCHBISHOP OF YORK**   Ash Wednesday presents us with some realism about our human nature and about the mess we make of things – through our own fault and through our own sheer sinfulness and wickedness. I think that has to be recognised, and that is part of what is set before us on Ash Wednesday.

- **BRIAN HOARE, FORMER PRESIDENT OF THE METHODIST CONFERENCE**   It is only in recent years that I've come to appreciate the value and importance of fasting – though I can't say even now that it's a spiritual discipline I practise very regularly. Ash Wednesday, however, reminds us of the reason for that sort of discipline, marking as it does the beginning of Lent and pointing us to the hardships and temptations Jesus subsequently faced in the wilderness. For him, what we call Ash Wednesday was the start of a period of inner wrestling with questions about the real nature of his calling and ministry. For me, it is a day which challenges me to sort out my own priorities, to resist the pull of self and sin, and to give myself wholly to discovering and obeying the will of God for my life.

- **PROFESSOR JOHN POLKINGHORNE FRS** Lent is about facing reality. If you go to an Ash Wednesday service and a cross is made on your forehead with ashes, the priest says, 'Dust you are, and to dust you shall return.' That sounds a pretty bleak, grim message but of course it is a real message. It tells us that there is death in the world and we need to face that fact. It is not the ultimate fact about the world, because the ultimate fact about the world is God and God's love which is stronger than death. So I think Lent is about seeing things as they are – opening our eyes to reality.

- **DAVID KONSTANT, ROMAN CATHOLIC BISHOP OF LEEDS** It is interesting that the prayers for Ash Wednesday talk about 'entering this joyful season'. It is a *joyful* season precisely because in seeking forgiveness we discover the real joy of repentance – which of us hasn't been happy when we've been able to say, 'I'm sorry'? And again, speaking from the Roman Catholic tradition, which of us hasn't been to Confession – received the Sacrament of Reconciliation – and not felt a wonderful sense of release and joy and peace?

On Temptation

- **DAVID HOPE** The account of the temptation in the wilderness is a focusing of the fact that Christ himself was tempted as we are.

- **JOHN POLKINGHORNE** Jesus came to lead a truly human life, and a truly human life necessarily involves perplexity – sorting out what is the right thing to do. The epistle to the Hebrews says a lot about that. Jesus is like us, he is able to help us, he is able to be our High Priest, because he knows what it is like to be human; he knows the problems . . . In Luke's account it says that the devil leaves him 'until an opportune time'. He is going to come back. Jesus hasn't won once for all in the wilderness. When you read that, you think about Gethsemane and the bitter temptation and difficulty that is portrayed there –

one of the deepest and most holy scenes in the Gospels.

- **DAVID KONSTANT**   Everybody has 'wilderness' experiences. How do I cope with them? In a variety of ways – by talking to friends, and by grumbling! Prayer is another way in which some of the really black moments can be relieved. I find the celebration of the liturgy an enormously powerful way to lift the cloud of sadness or whatever it is. And seeking forgiveness is another source – the discernment of self under the influence of prayer and the Spirit. The Psalmist's injunction to 'Be still and know that I am God' is the best medicine of the lot. In other words, it is discerning God in my life more clearly.

On the Bible

- **FIONA CASTLE**   I had always thought that the Bible was a bit of a boring history book . . . and suddenly after that [her dramatic conversion experience] it started to make sense and it started to be a handbook for life. I have never gone through a problem since where I haven't found the answer through reading God's Word. It is not always the answer I want to hear, because it is quite tough, but I know that it is right and that it works.

Questions for Groups

1   Have you been in a personal 'wilderness'? Did your faith help and sustain you? How? (After discussion you might find it helpful to read, or hear again on the cassette, Bishop David Konstant's comments.)

2   With Archbishop David Hope's warning in mind, spend 3–5 minutes on beginning to set yourself a realistic discipline for next Lent (if possible, write it down). This might involve: prayer, fasting or other abstinence, Bible reading, other reading, group study, almsgiving, campaigning for justice, visiting . . .

   (a) Share this with the group, together with any warnings or encouragements based on previous experience.

   (b) What do you hope to achieve through this discipline?

   (c) What might we learn from our Muslim neighbours, who fast very strictly during Ramadan?

3 Do you share Bishop David Konstant's view that Lent should be a *joyful* season?

4 Are there any other points on the cassette or in the text which you wish to discuss?

5 Re-read the checklist of Lenten dangers. Do you feel the force of these?

6 As you struggle with temptation, are you encouraged to think of Jesus struggling too, as 'one of us' (i.e. our brother and fellow-struggler, as well as our Great High Priest)? Or does this approach 'reduce' or insult him, in your view?

7 'At once the Spirit sent him out into the desert' (Mark 1:12). What does this tell us about our discipleship? (You might listen again to Fiona Castle's reflection on this.)

8 The language of battle was very familiar to earlier generations of Christians, e.g. 'Fight the good fight with all thy might'. Does such language still have force and relevance – or is it out-dated?

9 Jesus quoted the Scriptures and several contributors spoke of the importance of the Bible in their own experience.
  (a) If you could take only two Bible passages with you on to a desert island, which would you choose and why?
  (b) What would you say to a young person who asked why he/she should start reading the Bible, and asked for advice on how to begin?
  (c) Discuss attitudes to the Bible expressed on the cassette.

10 Some people are self-disciplined to the point of rigidity. Others have far too little self-discipline. Score yourself on a scale of 0–10. Perhaps give scores to one or two other group members, too (with their permission!).

    0   1   2   3   4   5   6   7   8   9   10
    No self-discipline   Too rigid an
                                          approach to life

  (a) Share your scores in the group – do you agree with each other's perceptions?
  (b) Discuss in the group how you can help one another to move up or down the scale.

SESSION 3: PALM SUNDAY

Near the end of his three years in the public eye, Jesus faced a crucial decision. Should he return home, to the safety of Galilee? Or should he go on to Jerusalem and to conflict? In his Gospel, Luke tells us that 'Jesus resolutely set out for Jerusalem'. That decision led to his death.

In Mark's Gospel we find a refrain on Jesus' lips: 'The Son of Man must suffer.' And in John's Gospel, Jesus refers to his death as his 'hour'. Everything he taught and did led up to his climactic death. This is seen most clearly in the dramatic events of the last week of his life.

The week began with his entry into Jerusalem. Jesus timed this to coincide with the great Jewish festival of Passover, when Jerusalem was teeming with pilgrims. His reputation ensured a large crowd. Jesus rode on a humble donkey, fulfilling the prophecy of Zechariah 9:9.

> Rejoice greatly, O Daughter of Zion!
> Shout, Daughter of Jerusalem!
> See, your king comes to you,
> righteous and having salvation,
> gentle and riding on a donkey . . .

Here was no worldly king, coming in glittering style to impress and command. Here was the Prince of Peace, riding in great humility. The crowds greeted him with shouts: 'Hosanna', which means 'Save now'. They scattered coats and palm branches on the road. That fateful day is now kept by Christians as 'Palm Sunday', the beginning of the most solemn and holy week in the entire Christian calendar.

Liberation Theology

Palm Sunday highlights a wide range of Christian themes and we cover several of these on the cassette. In the text we concentrate on Jesus' conflict with the religious and secular authorities. This began when he rode into Jerusalem, entered the Temple and overturned the tables. It resulted in the most famous act of washing in all history, as Pontius Pilate tried to distance himself from the decision to crucify Jesus.

In modern times the conflict between Christian and secular leaders has been focused famously in liberation theology – a controversial movement which has influenced the Church world-wide. At a conference held in Columbia in 1968, some Roman Catholic bishops from Latin America insisted that the starting point for theological reflection must be the situation of the poor. Liberation theology was born. At the forefront of this movement is the belief that the God of the Bible is on the side of the down-trodden and marginalised. Liberation theologians remind us that:

- God heard the cry of the children of Israel when they were enslaved in Egypt.
- The Old Testament prophets were passionate in demanding social justice.
- Mary's song (the Magnificat) is revolutionary: God 'has filled the hungry with good things but has sent the rich away empty' (Luke 1:53).
- Jesus showed particular concern for the poor and those on the edge of society.
- Christianity is a 'this-worldly' religion, concerned with the welfare of mind and body as well as redemption of the soul.

The Bible is seen as a very practical book, concerned with freedom from physical oppression *and* freedom of the human spirit. Liberation theology is concerned with reflection, action ('praxis') and raising the awareness of poor people concerning issues of justice. Something of its mood is caught in these statements:

As a sign of the liberation of humankind and history, the Church

*itself in its concrete existence ought to be a place of liberation . . .
The point is not to survive, but to serve. The rest will be given.*
(Gustavo Gutiérrez)

The poor man, the other, reveals the totally Other to us.
(Gutiérrez)

Theology has to stop explaining the world and start reforming it. (J.
Migguez-Bonino)

*The Church in liberation theology is rooted in a faith in God and
an option for the poor.* (Marilyn J. Legge)

*The God of the Future is the crucified God who submerges himself
in a world of misery. God is found on the crosses of the oppressed
rather than in beauty, power or wisdom.* (D.D. Webster)

On Religion and Politics

- **BRIAN HOARE**   During the nine years of my ministry on
  the staff at Cliff College, I was responsible for leading pre-Easter
  missions to a wide variety of churches. I find it hard to think of
  Palm Sunday (the day our mission weeks ended) without it
  evoking memories of those events. The theme is particularly
  appropriate for such a time of outreach, for the original Palm
  Sunday was a very public event as Jesus rode into Jerusalem
  and was popularly acclaimed as the Messiah, the King of Israel.
  For me, the Palm Sunday challenge to make Jesus king is
  well expressed in the words a Cliff evangelist used to sing:
  'To do his will, whatever cost; to yield to him alone; in every
  detail of your life, let Jesus have the throne.' *Singing* it is the easy
  bit!
- **DAVID HOPE**   The Church must be involved in politics in
  the sense that politics is to do with people's lives. Christianity is
  not a wholly spiritualised religion. The whole point about the
  incarnation – about Christmas – is that God is intimately
  involved in the lives and well-being of people.
- **DAVID KONSTANT**   Religion isn't just a matter of the

spiritual. The simplest definition of religion is in the letter of St James, where he says that true religion is looking after orphans and widows. You cannot get more direct than that – you cannot divide the spiritual from the material.

- **FIONA CASTLE**   I believe that Christians should be present in every part of life and that we should be, as Jesus said, 'salt and light' in a dark and tasteless world. We have to enable other people to see that there is another way to go about life and that it does work.

On Ambition

- **DAVID HOPE**   (On ecclesiastical titles, bishops' palaces and other trappings of high office.) One of the things I tend to question . . . is the fact that you are de-personalised in these sorts of jobs. It seems to me to be wholly against what we understand in terms of relationships within the Christian body . . . There is a sense in which I believe it is a stumbling block to the Gospel. The Church as a pilgrim Church – a Church on the move – needs to be travelling a good deal lighter and with greater simplicity. I do think that as we look towards a new millennium there is perhaps some room for what I might term a new asceticism within the Church.

- **DAVID KONSTANT**   The term 'bishop' is a description. It describes the work that I have to do. Of course, if a person is remote, inaccessible, on a pedestal, refuses to see people – yes, there is a barrier there. I hope we avoid that.

- **GORDON WILSON**   I have two good friends in Enniskillen who promise me that the moment they hear me say something or see me do something that they know is not the real Gordon Wilson, they will tell me. And I know they will. Because my strength – if I have any strength – is my simplicity; the fact that I speak from the heart.

- **JOHN POLKINGHORNE**   I think it is impossible for the Christian not to have ambition. What we need to try to have is the right ambition. That is what Augustine said: what we need is 'the right desire' – to seek to serve people and to serve God and not just to glorify ourselves. There is a right ambition which is to find the place in which you can use the gifts which God has given you; that must be the right thing to do.

On Holy Communion

- **DAVID HOPE**   That is the work of God – part of the profligacy of God – that in spite of the mess that I make of myself or of it all, God continues to give endlessly, recklessly, and I think Holy Communion is a demonstration in our midst of that gift.
- **GORDON WILSON**   To the question: 'What goes through your mind when you receive Holy Communion?' Gordon replied: 'The fact that I am a sinner; the fact that I need forgiveness for my sins. The fact that it is freely offered and opportunity given for me to repent – because repentance and forgiveness are interwoven. You cannot have one without the other. So that is what goes through my mind. I feel a better and cleaner man coming back down the aisle, than I do going up.'

On Obedience

- **FIONA CASTLE**   If people think that life is going to be a bed of roses they haven't read the Bible, because Jesus himself actually said, 'In the world you will have trouble, but have courage because I have overcome the world.' And I always think of that and St Paul saying, 'I am content to have everything or nothing.' I feel that is much more realistic than expecting everything to suddenly go well for you and to be prosperous and have loads of money. I think that is incredibly unimportant in life. The way we will be fulfilled is through doing what God wants us to do and being obedient, not by being affluent.
- **JOHN POLKINGHORNE**   When we pray, we are doing two things. We are saying to God – look, you act in the world; you also allow us to act in the world. I want to act with you. We would like to align our wills with your will to bring about what you want. Second, we are telling God what it is we really want. Although God isn't a heavenly Father Christmas who gives us whatever we ask for, he does take seriously what we tell him, what is our heart's desire.

Questions for Groups

1   Have you met anyone whom you would describe as truly proud or humble? Describe that person's strengths and weaknesses.

2   'In humility consider others better than yourselves' (Phil. 2:3).
    (a) Is this realistic?
    (b) Can you be humble *and* be a positive person with strong opinions?

3   David Hope, reflecting on ecclesiastical titles, bishops' palaces, etc., said: 'There is a sense in which I believe it is a stumbling block to the Gospel. The Church as a pilgrim Church – a Church on the move – needs to be travelling a good deal lighter and with greater simplicity . . . There is perhaps some room for what I might term a new asceticism within the Church.'
    (a) Do you agree with him?
    (b) How can this be achieved?

4   'Those who say that religion has nothing to do with politics do not know what religion means' (Gandhi). 'Are not Religion and Politics the same Thing? Brotherhood is Religion' (William Blake). 'The Christian Church is the one organisation in the world that exists purely for the benefit of non-members' (William Temple). 'I find myself, unlike the contemporary Church, thinking more and more about the next world and less and less about the third world' (Alexander Dru).
    (a) Give each of these statements a score on a 0–5 scale (0 = bad, 5 = excellent).
    (b) Share your scores and your reasons.
    (c) Discuss any points about liberation theology in the text above.

5   Christians were involved in the conspiracy to assassinate Hitler. Can you think of any situation in modern Britain where you would contemplate breaking the law of the land, in obedience to the law of God?

6   'Christianity is not a wholly spiritualised religion' (Archbishop David Hope). 'Religion isn't just a matter of the spiritual' (Bishop David Konstant). 'We should be, as Jesus said, "salt

and light" in a dark and tasteless world' (Fiona Castle).

(a) Do you agree/disagree with the above statements?

(b) What might they mean for you and your church, in practical terms?

7   Two young Christians confide in you that they seem to get little out of Holy Communion. They find it hard to concentrate and – unlike Gordon Wilson, David Konstant and David Hope on the cassette – they feel no different after receiving. How would you respond?

8   'Prayer changes things.' Does it? (You might wish to listen again to John Polkinghorne's comments on the tape at some point during your discussion.)

9   Gordon Wilson had friends who agreed to talk honestly with him about his conduct and attitudes. Do you have friends – or perhaps a counsellor or spiritual director – with whom you can share at a deep level? Explain the benefits of this.

10 Should Christians have ambitions? What are yours?

SESSION 4: GOOD FRIDAY

In Lyons in AD 177, the authorities tried to stamp out the Church. Eusebius recorded the way in which they set about 'persuading' the Christians to disown their God and swear by the pagan idols. Blandina, he reported, wore out her tormentors with her endurance. Eventually she was killed by a bull. 'And so,' wrote Eusebius, 'she travelled herself along the same path of conflicts as they [her fellow-martyrs] did, and hastened to them rejoicing and exulting in her departure.'

The peace and serenity, and the sense of the presence of God displayed by Blandina, is characteristic of the Christian martyrs. It is in sharp contrast to the death of Jesus himself. In the Passion narratives in the Gospels:

- We find a *lack* of serenity: 'He began to be deeply distressed and troubled.'
- We find a *lack* of peace: 'My soul is overwhelmed with sorrow.'
- We find a *desire for escape*: '*Abba*, Father . . . take this cup from me.'
- We even find a *sense of abandonment* by God, as Jesus quotes the opening line of Psalm 22: 'My God, my God, why have you forsaken me?'

For those who died *for* Jesus Christ – a constant sense of the presence of God. For Jesus as *he* died – a sense of abandonment by God and of utter loneliness. The martyrs faced death willingly; Jesus shrank from it.

Add to this the fact that those who followed Jesus to martyrdom drew their inspiration from his death, and we have a remarkable puzzle. It is a puzzle to which the New Testament gives a solution. The answer given there is that, for Jesus, *there was an extra factor*. The martyrs suffered physically; Jesus suffered physically, emotionally *and spiritually*, as he experienced separation from God the Father for the first time in his life.

The martyrs bore *pain* for him; he bore *sin* for them. Not only their own sin, but the sin of the whole world. And it is sin which separates from God – hence the cry of abandonment from the cross. All this was summed up by John the Baptist when he referred to Jesus as 'the Lamb of God, who takes away the sin of the world' (John 1:29).

Why it was necessary for Jesus to die to win our salvation is a deep mystery. Indeed, St Paul admits that the notion of a man dying on a cross to save the world appears very foolish (1 Cor. 1:18–25). It cannot be fully understood: it can only be proclaimed – and believed or denied. But this mystery sheds light upon, and brings meaning to, countless lives. The New Testament probes the significance of the death of Christ. We may attempt to sum up its significance under four headings.

1   ***The cross reveals the depth of human sin***   As Jesus died, the land was covered in daytime darkness. It was as though heaven itself was saying: this is the most dreadful day of all – for pride, greed, jealousy and hatred appear to have triumphed. But God took those evil actions and attitudes and used them as the raw materials from which to quarry our salvation.

2   ***The cross reveals the depth of God's love***   Jesus chose to submit himself to human wickedness. So the power of God is seen in symbols of weakness: a borrowed manger for his birth and a wooden cross at his death. Here is power kept in check, power handed over, power utterly controlled by love. Jesus' body was broken like bread and his life was poured out like wine, for the forgiveness of sins.

3   ***The cross reveals the way back to God***   On the cross Jesus cried out, 'It is finished.' The Greek word (*tetelestai*) carries a triumphant ring. Not 'It's all over', but '*It is accomplished*'. According to the Bible, only his death, the death of the Son of God, could break down the barriers of rebellion and indifference which separate us from God and from one another. So we call that terrible day *Good* Friday. The day was terrible, but

the fruit of the day is beautiful. As Jesus died, the curtain in the Temple was torn in two from top to bottom – a dramatic sign of new access into the presence of God.

4   ***The cross reveals the demands of Christian discipleship*** 'Follow me,' said Jesus. Then he took the road to crucifixion. As baptism indicates (Rom. 6:4), following Christ always involves a sort of death. Paradoxically, Jesus insists that the cross is also about life: 'For whoever wants to save his life will lose it, but whoever loses his life for me and for the gospel will save it' (Mark 8:35).

- **DAVID KONSTANT**   We are people who need signs and realities. It is not enough for someone just to forgive someone else in their heart. They want to see the person smile, they want to hear the person saying, 'It's all right, I forgive you; I still love you.' This is what God does continually. He says, 'I do forgive you – even if a mother could forget her child I could never forget you.' But, in the end, the one thing that really convinces us that God is on our side totally is that he sent his own Son, to convince us that we are loved, that we are forgiven, that we are made whole, that we are saved.

- **BRIAN HOARE**   Some twenty years ago I heard Annie Vallotton (the artist who did those marvellous drawings in the Good News Bible) speak at a big international congress in Brussels. What feeling she conveyed by a few simple pen strokes on an overhead projector as she spoke! For me her illustration of Romans 6:6 speaks volumes about the meaning of Good Friday: Jesus' death on the cross frees us from the burden of our sin. That truth expressed comprehensively (Christ died for all) has a wonderful breadth about it, but it's easy to overlook the personal application. As a school teacher I sometimes had to follow up a general command to the whole class by saying, 'And that includes you!' Perhaps God needs to say that to us about what Jesus did on the cross.

- **DAVID HOPE**   I am part of the human race which has built into it a fault line. The cross is the demonstration – that and the resurrection – that God has not given up on us and that things can be different. That once-upon-a-time event becomes a once-and-for-*all*-time event, and that is very relevant to me and to our human condition here and now.

- **JOHN POLKINGHORNE**
  In that lonely figure in the dark, in the spent force of a deserted man dying on a cross, they see not the ultimate triumph of evil or futility but the only source of hope for mankind. 'God was in Christ reconciling the world to himself' (2 Cor. 5:19) . . . The crucifixion was not something which got out of hand, a tragic mistake which marred an otherwise wonderful life. On the contrary, it was the inevitable fulfilment of the life, purposed by God.

The reason we call it Good Friday is, I think, the deep mystery that there we see God himself opening his arms on the cross, in Christ, to accept and be part of human suffering and by that acceptance to triumph over it . . . Good Friday is full of darkness and the terrible cry of dereliction – and Jesus really dies. That is part of God's acceptance of the suffering of the world, so that he may redeem the suffering of the world.

- **FIONA CASTLE**   During Roy's illness, I suppose you could call doubt the time when we felt that God was far away. Again I would have to turn to the time when I really did doubt that there was any purpose to life at all, and twenty-one years ago God brought such purpose to my life that, even though life is tough, I have this deep, deep-down conviction that it is real.

  I would never underestimate the value of prayer and I really believe that although perhaps prayer was not answered the way we would have liked to see it answered, I honestly believe that through the prayers of the faithful people who prayed for Roy, the battle was won in the heavenlies – because Roy was strong, he was faithful right to the end. I believe that through prayer we were given opportunities to share our faith.

- **GORDON WILSON**   There are two kinds of forgiveness and they are intertwined. There is man's forgiveness of man and there is God's forgiveness of man. Since the guys whom I forgave haven't repented . . . unless they repent to God they are going to finish up in hell. And the same applies to me. I have got to repent as well or I am going to finish up in hell.

Questions for Groups

1   As you listen to the audio-tape, jot down any points with which you strongly agree or disagree. Share and discuss these.

2   Ask three people to read, from the Gospels, the seven recorded statements of Jesus from the Cross. Take a couple of quiet minutes to jot down a comment on *one* or *two* of them, then share these comments with the group.

3   (a) Your Buddhist visitor (the one who asked about Christmas) asks, 'What happened on Good Friday?' What would you say?

   (b) He is surprised that you call it 'Good Friday' and asks, 'Have you Christians no feelings?' How would you respond?

4   'Forgive us our sins as we forgive those who sin against us.' 'Father, forgive them . . .' (Luke 23:34). 'I realised that anger and bitterness are not good. They eat you up and you could become very bitter yourself . . . I bear them [his daughter's killers] no ill-will' (Gordon Wilson).

   (a) Was Gordon Wilson right, in your view?

   (b) Share your own struggles with forgiveness.

   (c) What would you say to someone who said:
      – I can't forgive him/her for what he/she did.
      – I can't forgive myself for doing that.
      – I can't forgive God for allowing this to happen.

5   Jesus said, 'Take up your cross and follow me.' What might this mean, in practical day-to-day terms, for you today? You might wish to use the following paragraph to get you going. 'Follow me,' said Jesus. Then he took the road to crucifixion. As baptism indicates, following Christ always involves a sort of death. He died *for* us; we are called to die (a kind of death) *with* him. This means holding Christian standards in a world which often rejects those standards. It means following Jesus in a world which is often indifferent towards him. It means showing compassion, when indifference is so much easier. Paradoxically,

Jesus insists that the cross is also about life. 'For whoever wants to save his life will lose it, but whoever loses his life for me and for the gospel will save it' (Mark 8:35).

6 (a) A young person asks, 'How can Jesus' death *then*, save me *now*?' What would you say?

   (b) Artists sometimes set the crucifixion in their own period and setting – a declaration that Christ must not be tamed by religion nor trapped in history. How might the crucifixion be portrayed effectively today?

7 Singly or in pairs, compose a devotional prayer (like St Richard's prayer, below) based on the cross. Use them next week – or publish them in your church newsletter/magazine.

8 Lord MacLeod of Iona wrote:

> I simply argue that the cross be raised again at the centre of the marketplace as well as on the steeple of the church. I am recovering the claim that Jesus was not crucified in a cathedral between two candles, but on a cross between two thieves; on the town garbage heap; at a crossroads so cosmopolitan that they had to write his title in Hebrew and Latin and in Greek ... at the kind of place where cynics talk smut, and thieves curse, and soldiers gamble. Because this is where he died. And this is what he died about. And that is where churchmen ought to be; and what churchmen should be about.

What might this mean in practical terms for you, your group and your church(es)?

9 Replay the quotation from 'Woodbine Willie' at the end of 'Good Friday' on the cassette. Then read the following declaration by John Stott: 'I could never myself believe in God, if it were not for the cross ... In the real world of pain, how could one worship a God who was immune from it?'

   (a) Do these words reflect your view?

   (b) Have the sufferings of Christ kept you going during dark times?

St Richard's Prayer
(for Question 8 and to end the meeting)

Thanks be to thee, my Lord Jesus Christ, for all the benefits which thou hast given me, for all the pains and insults which thou has borne for me. O most merciful Redeemer, Friend and Brother: may I see thee more clearly, love thee more dearly, and follow thee more nearly, day by day. Amen.

SESSION 5: EASTER

Three years after the Russian Revolution of 1917, a great anti-God rally was arranged in Kiev. The powerful orator Bukharin was sent from Moscow, and for an hour he demolished the Christian faith with argument, abuse and ridicule. At the end there was silence. Then questions were invited.

A priest of the Russian Orthodox Church stood up and uttered three words – the ancient liturgical greeting used on Easter Sunday. 'Christ is risen.' At once, the entire assembly gave the joyful response: 'He is risen indeed.' A devastating moment for an atheist politician, who made no reply. (Source: Bishop Lesslie Newbigin.)

Of course, this does not prove the resurrection. Indeed, Good Friday gives a dramatic reminder that majorities can be terribly wrong. So the question persists. Dead men don't rise; so why believe that this particular dead man did rise? The answer is to be found in the uniqueness of Jesus and in the power of God. Jesus was too good and too great to be held by death. Having defeated sin on the cross he went on to defeat sin's first cousin. But Jesus did not raise himself. The New Testament asserts that it was God the Father who raised Jesus from the dead. At the beginning of time, God created the universe out of nothing. Now he brings life out of death.

Easy to say but – for many people in the modern world – hard to believe. And for some people in the ancient world, too. At the end of St Luke's Gospel we read that, 'They still did not believe it because of joy and amazement' (Luke 24:41). The disciples had visited the empty tomb; and they had seen the risen Lord. Still they disbelieved. Not because they were stubborn and disobedient – but because they were overwhelmed. It seemed too good to be true. They disbelieved . . . *because of joy*!

We don't know what happened in the tomb on that first Easter morning. No one saw Jesus rise from the dead. Perhaps no human being could have survived exposure to such awesome energy. Whatever the reason, the resurrection happened without human witnesses. Shortly afterwards, people visited the tomb and found it empty. The first visitor thought that someone had removed Jesus' body. Hence Mary Magdalene's poignant request to the gardener: 'Sir, if you have carried him away, tell me where you have put him' (John 20:15).

But according to St John, Mary was not talking to a gardener. She was talking to a carpenter. It was Jesus himself, risen from the dead. This illustrates two important features of the New Testament account. First the empty tomb; then the appearances of the risen Lord. Taken together, these events convinced the first disciples that God had raised Jesus from the dead. Their conviction was tested in the crucible. They suffered for it. Some died for it. But their belief could not be shaken.

This is very impressive. People will not die for their *inventions*. They will, and do, die for their *convictions*. One thing is absolutely certain. When the first disciples claimed to have seen the risen Lord, they meant what they said. The evidence for the resurrection has convinced some remarkable modern witnesses, too, including the *Jewish* scholar Pinchas Lapide. He wrote a book entitled *The Resurrection of Jesus* and said: 'I accept the resurrection of Jesus, not as an invention of the community of disciples, but as a historical event.'

The joyful good news of Easter which Christians are called to share has two facets

* **Jesus is alive**   Jesus is active in our world and in our lives. Not simply through his marvellous teaching. Not only by his matchless example. But by *his living presence*. If we allow him to do so, he will inspire us, challenge us, guide us, renew us.
* **Death is dead**   As the anti-Christian philosopher Nietzsche observed, we are 'the brotherhood of death'. Mark Twain gave this a characteristic twist: 'No-one gets out alive.' In the face of this terrifying fact, we rejoice that Jesus is 'the resurrection and the life'. In other words, while the first Easter story describes a unique and wonderful event, it is a highly *significant* event too.

Easter has enormous implications.

The New Testament describes the resurrection of Jesus as 'the first fruits' of a great harvest. *We* are that harvest. Because God raised Jesus, he will raise us. Because Jesus defeated death, we shall inherit eternal life. To change the picture: by his resurrection Jesus flung wide open the gates of Glory. We are invited to join the vibrant life of heaven.

- **DAVID KONSTANT** (speaking on Luke 24:13–35, the road to Emmaus) All of us doubt from time to time, and here is a gradual unfolding of the Word of God by the Word made flesh, who has died and was risen. 'Were not our hearts burning within us as he unfolded for us the meaning of the Scriptures?' There is that. There is also, 'We knew him in the breaking of the bread.' There is a rich symbolism and a deep reality in that and the way they suddenly rushed back when they realised who had been with them.

  When we die we are being asked to lay down our life. We are not being asked to be passive in our dying, but actually to say, 'Amen. I give myself to you.' That is the meaning of the resurrection for me. It is a promise of eternal life.

- **JOHN POLKINGHORNE** It is a very bad mistake to be too spiritually minded about things. Human beings are a mixture of matter and spirit. Matter matters. It is not our destiny to become angels. We are to be resurrected, to have new bodies – glorified bodies, as Jesus was given his body. The empty tomb tells us that in Jesus, in Christ, there is a future not only for humankind, but for matter. The whole world is going to die, but God cares for the whole of his creation and there is a destiny for matter in Christ Jesus as there is a destiny for humankind. That's very important for me.

- **BRIAN HOARE** Of all the Christian festivals, I think Easter is my favourite. When I was a minister in Hull it was our custom to end our early Easter morning service by going outside the church to sing the final hymn with its confident chorus: 'Up from the grave he arose ... Alleluia! Christ arose!' The realisation that we don't simply look back to a historical figure whose life provides us with a wonderful example, but have a living Saviour whom we can know and serve personally today, blows my mind! One of my favourite Easter texts (Rom. 6:4) explains that 'just as Christ was raised from the dead . . . so we too may live a new life'. That's certainly a truth to be lived – and shared with the communities in which we live and work.

- **DAVID HOPE**　God did not and will not give up on us. Death is not the end. We have been created to enjoy each other in the presence of God for ever. There is a glorious future ahead of us.

- **DAME CICELY SAUNDERS**　quoted Augustine's *City of God*. 'We shall rest and we shall see; we shall see and we shall love; we shall love and we shall praise; in the end which is no end.'

　　On *Euthanasia*, she commented:

　I don't think that we are a society which could be trusted with such a law. As an old lady wrote to *The Times*: 'Human nature being what it is, euthanasia wouldn't be voluntary for long.'

- **FIONA CASTLE**　When Roy died I was really able to release him to God. It was such a relief because I had been praying, 'God, how much longer can you make him put up with this suffering? You know it's not fair.' So in a sense there was a huge relief because there was no quality of life there, so in a sense it was wonderful when he did die.

- **GORDON WILSON**　I am never unaware of God's presence. I know he is there, I know he cares for me. I know his love surrounds me. I am sure of these things and that assurance means that I don't worry about him not being there. I was not afraid and am not afraid to die, because I'm back where I started. I like to think that I will be among friends.

As scientist Arthur Peacocke reflects on the puzzle of how we might be resurrected, he draws an analogy from computers. He suggests that 'the pattern in our brains which constitutes the essential you and me' is rather like software. 'We know that software programmes can be embodied in many different kinds of hardware – and yet the software is real enough.'

Historian Gillian Evans considers the modern concern that heaven will be 'beautiful but dull'. She affirms that 'we should be envisaging a freedom from the confinement of time and space which will make it possible for us to be with all our friends at once and individually, to be enjoying an infinite variety of things as we choose, without delay or hurry, crowding or isolation. It is something new, a new quality of life.' (From John Young, *Teach Yourself Christianity*, Hodder & Stoughton.)

I suggest that you tackle this quiz and discuss findings before listening to the cassette and tackling the Questions for Groups.

Easter Quiz

1   What colour were ancient Easter eggs often painted – and why?
    (a) Yellow (b) Red (c) Blue (d) Green
2   The goldsmith who created the most famous Easter eggs was:
    (a) Russian? (b) French? (c) British? (d) Hungarian?
3   Why Easter eggs?
4   Which Gospel(s) contain(s) the story of the appearance of Jesus to the disciples at Emmaus?
    (a) Matthew (b) Mark (c) Luke (d) John
5   In a MORI poll in 1991 what percentage of British people did not know why Easter is celebrated?
    (a) 5% (b) 10% (c) 35% (d) 55%
6   Why do most Christians keep Sunday special – not Saturday (the Sabbath) like the Jews?
7   Why isn't the date of Easter fixed, like Christmas?
8   Which Gospel(s) has/have more than one possible ending?
9   Which Gospel(s) contain(s) the story of the appearance of

Jesus to Mary Magdalene in the garden?

10 Of which religion are the scholars who made these statements?
   – 'It is still very important, in a sceptical and often hostile culture, that the Easter story should stand up to attack – no easy matter at a distance of almost two thousand years. But stand up it does.'
   (a) Christian (b) Jewish (c) Hindu (d) Buddhist
   – 'I accept the resurrection of Jesus not as an invention of the community of disciples, but as a historical event.'
   (a) Christian (b) Jewish (c) Hindu (d) Buddhist

Answers to Easter Quiz

1 Red – to recall Christ's blood.
2 Peter Carl Fabergé (1846–1920) was Russian.
3 They remind us that Jesus rose to new life from a dark tomb.
4 Luke.
5 35%.
6 To celebrate Jesus' resurrection. Every Sunday is a mini Easter.
7 Easter is based on Passover – observed at full moon.
8 Mark.
9 John.
10 Christian (Bishop John Austin Baker); Jewish (Professor Pinchas Lapide).

Questions for Groups

1 (a) Do you think about your own death?
   occasionally/frequently/never
   (b) Does a belief in heaven and eternal life, comfort and encourage you?
2 Have you planned your own funeral?
   (a) Which hymns/readings/music do you want?
   (b) What 'mood' do you want? (joyful/sad/ . . . ?)
   (c) Do you think such planning is a good or bad thing?
3 'Pray for me, and I shall pray for you and all your friends, that we may merrily meet in heaven' (words from St Thomas

More's last letter to his daughter, as he awaited execution under Henry VIII).

(a) Do you ever try to visualise heaven? How do you see it?

(b) Are Gillian Evans/Arthur Peacock helpful (see pp. 58–9)?

4   David Konstant and Gordon Wilson both speak with assurance about going to heaven. Some people feel that such assurance is presumptuous. Others feel that provided confidence about going to heaven is rooted in the promises of Jesus and the grace of God (rather than our own assumed goodness) it is presumptuous *not* to be certain. Where do you stand on this?

5   Discuss points on the cassette and/or in the text with which you strongly agree or disagree.

6   An atheist friend challenges you: 'How can you believe that Jesus died on the cross only to be raised to new life?' How would you reply? (You might listen again to scientist John Polkinghorne on the cassette.)

7   Read aloud and each write one sentence on both of the following passages. Share your sentences on (a) before listening to passage (b).

(a) The road to Emmaus (Luke 24:28–35)

(b) Mary Magdalene in the Garden (John 20:10–18)

8   The disciples in Emmaus 'knew him in the breaking of bread'. Your Buddhist friend asks, 'What does Holy Communion mean to you?' What would you say?

9   Listen again to the Albert Schweitzer quotation in the summary on the cassette (or see p. 99).

(a) Do you have a sense of being 'accompanied' through life by the Risen Lord?

(b) Are you 'learning in your own experience who he is'?

(c) Does the passage ring true in your experience?

You may wish to close the meeting by reading one of the Summaries on pp. 24 and 129 (using various voices).

SESSION 6: PENTECOST

Pentecost is sometimes called 'the birthday of the Church'. The Holy Spirit came in power, and the prophecy of Joel and the promise of Jesus (Acts 1:8) were fulfilled. From a large amount of material on the Holy Spirit, we will select five features.

1   **The Holy Spirit is practical**   The Church needs a rich variety of gifts. It needs administrators, helpers and encouragers. It needs prophets, evangelists, healers and teachers. No single Christian has all the gifts. God equips his Church for worship, witness and loving service by scattering his gifts around. Quite literally in the Greek, he 'dollops out' his gifts among his people. These gifts are given to us by God 'for the common good' (1 Cor. 12:7). My gifts are not 'mine' for personal use and advantage. They are to be shared and used within the body of Christ – and to equip us to serve our troubled and divided world.

The Roman Catholic theologian Karl Rahner sums up: 'They [the gifts of the Spirit] are never all given to one individual. They may – like healing powers or speaking in tongues – be quite extraordinary and even spectacular in nature. But they can also be almost secular, everyday capabilities, up to the point of good cash administration of a parish or community.'

2   **The Holy Spirit is creative**   God wants to grow a lovely harvest within our lives. St Paul names nine different qualities: love, joy, peace, patience, kindness, goodness, faithfulness, gentleness and self-control (Gal. 5:22–3). Each one of these 'fruits of the Spirit' should become apparent in every believer. (On the cassette, the Archbishop of York comments on the connection between the more dramatic manifestations of the Spirit's presence and that harvest of love, joy, peace . . .)

3   **The Holy Spirit brings new life**   The Bible speaks about the

greatness of God. He is transcendent; awesome; enthroned in heaven. It speaks too about the closeness, or 'immanence' of God. He is with us *by his Spirit* – bringing strength, power and inspiration. This was summed up by Anglican monk Harry Williams: 'Being a Christian means . . . being people in whom his [Jesus'] life and character and power are manifest and energised . . . Christian experience is not so much a matter of imitating a leader . . . as accepting and receiving a new quality of life – a life infinitely more profound and dynamic and meaningful than human life without Christ.'

4   *The Holy Spirit breaks barriers*   That first Christian Pentecost was Babel in reverse. Human pride brought God's judgement, when men built the fabulous tower at Babel (Gen. 11). The result was division and a breakdown in communication. In contrast, on the day of Pentecost, people from different countries, with different languages, heard and understood the same message. In Christ, the curse of Babel gives way to the blessing of Pentecost. Division and conflict are (or should be) replaced by unity and harmony.

5   *The Spirit makes trouble!*   Jesus made it clear that there is nothing complicated about receiving God's Spirit. '. . . how much more will your Father in heaven give the Holy Spirit to those who ask him?' (Luke 11:13). If we invite the Spirit into our lives he *will* come – that is the promise of Jesus. But beware! He will come as a restless guest, not as a quiet, house-trained visitor. We have invited the *Holy* Spirit. He will touch areas of our lives which we have not submitted to God's will, for he wants to transform us into a living temple (1 Cor. 3:16). And the Spirit can be as troublesome within the Church as within individuals. New life can disturb old and settled customs!

• **JOHN POLKINGHORNE**   If we are going to live a Christian life we have to live it by God's grace and strength and in God's presence. The Holy Spirit is the almost hidden presence of God at work in our lives and in the world . . . The Holy Spirit is self-effacing. The role of the Holy Spirit is to bear witness to Christ so in that sense he is the Spirit of Christ in our

hearts, saying 'Father' in the way that Jesus said 'Father' to God.
So the Holy Spirit's job is to point away from himself to Christ.
In that sense he is the Spirit of Christ, but he is not the same as
Christ.

The Holy Spirit may sometimes give very striking gifts to
people, but in other places he is at work very quietly and silently
in people's lives. I think that is how he works in my life. God
does work in strange ways – in un-English and un-Anglican
ways! That little experience [described on the cassette] has made
me cautious of being dismissive of people whose experiences
are radically different from my own rather staid way of life.

- **DAVID KONSTANT** I like the very powerful image at
Creation, with the Spirit hovering over the deep, which echoes
the Holy Spirit hovering over Mary at the time of her conception. And the image of a cleansing wind which blows through
my life and clears the cobwebs of doubt and unbelief, so that I
can see more clearly the way I should go. They say that at the
second Vatican Council they opened the windows so that the
Holy Spirit could actually get in and do something! Maybe that
is the case for all councils of the Church – and for all councils in
a family. It is the openness of the people there to the real
influence of the Holy Spirit.

We are talking about a total reversal of the Tower of Babel.
It is total unity we are concerned with – it is one of our prime
duties to discover a deeper unity. I am full of hope. I recognise
the huge problems there are: there is a long way to go before
we can say, 'We are one in the Spirit, we are one in the Lord.'
We are much more one in the Lord than we used to be. Insofar
as we are truly open to the Spirit, I believe we will become one
as a Christian family – not in our lifetime, perhaps, but in time.

- **BRIAN HOARE** It was at a student conference way back in
the 1950s that I first began to understand the meaning of
Pentecost, and subsequently to experience the power of the
Holy Spirit for myself. Since those days there has been growing
emphasis on the Spirit, and I rejoice in that, despite all the
accompanying problems and debates the topic has raised. At
least they are problems of life, not death. I once stood on the

great Akosombo Dam in Ghana during a time of drought and saw the words 'Minimum operating level' on the wall – but metres above the actual water level. It reminded me that we are all called to 'be filled with the Spirit'. That's the norm for a Christian. The grave danger is that we too often try to live below the minimum operating level!

- **FIONA CASTLE** I am fairly ecumenical myself, because I was born and brought up an Anglican; I went to an Anglo-Catholic boarding school; my two girls went to a Roman Catholic convent school; my son went to a Quaker school; and I now worship in a Baptist church! The Bible says we are all one in Christ Jesus. I get really sad when people start saying, 'Well, I wouldn't do it this way,' because I think we are focusing on the *dis*unifying points rather than the unifying points. Jesus himself said it is not *where* you worship but *how* you worship – that you worship in spirit and in truth. We need to focus on the fact that Jesus wants us to be one. If we are different denominations we are still there because we love Jesus. I heard a comment that someone who is fanatical is someone who loves Jesus more than you do! I want to be the most radical in that.

- **DAME CICELY SAUNDERS** Although I know that unity is meant to be very important, I think different ways of approach are just as important . . . differences are not nearly so important as what we have in common.

- **DAVID HOPE** The work of God's Spirit down the ages has always been somewhat extravagant and we have seen movements which have manifested extravagant signs and wonders . . . Well, so be it. The question to ask is – is that increasing in the individual, and in the Church as a whole, a greater sense of God's compassion, God's care, God's love? Equally the fruits of the Spirit are manifested in waiting, in silence, in the more contemplative aspects of life. It is not either one or the other . . . we gladly rejoice in all these things.

  I think we cannot be excused, any of us, from seeking to make a reality of Christ's prayer that we all be one. For the sake of the world, not as an end in itself. Because the Gospel message is weakened and undermined by the scandal of disunity.

Questions for Groups

1 Read aloud Karl Rahner's paragraph (p. 62). The gifts of the Spirit are spread around. No one has them all; everybody has at least one.
   (a) Which gift(s) do you think you have?
   (b) Which gift(s) would you like to have?
   (c) Which gifts do other group members have, in your view? List one gift for each group member.
   It might be interesting to share your ideas!

2 (a) Every Christian believer is required to cultivate every one of the fruits of the Spirit (look up Galatians 5:22–3). Pick out two of these qualities which you need to work on. Share your thoughts.
   (b) Read the passage about the Holy Spirit as troublemaker. How might this apply to you and your church?

3 Raise any points from the cassette and/or text with which you strongly agree/disagree.

4 Your Buddhist visitor attends church and hears you say, 'We believe in the Holy Spirit.' 'What is this Holy Spirit?' he asks. 'And how does God's Spirit relate to God's Son?' How would you reply?

5 We asked our distinguished contributors to name a book, a person and an experience, or series of experiences, which have been important for the formation of their Christian faith. (But, alas, had no extra space on the cassette.) What would you say in response to this question?

6 The charismatic renewal movement stresses the work of the Holy Spirit and is approved by some senior leaders in all the churches.
   (a) Do you have any experience of this movement?
   (b) Are you nervous about it? If so, why?
   (c) Are you enthusiastic about it? If so, why?

7 On the cassette, the Roman Catholic Bishop of Leeds seems very optimistic about Christian unity.
   (a) Is he right? Do you share his enthusiasm?
   (b) What practical action can you take to enhance unity – as an individual/a church/a discussion group/a group of churches?

    (c) What about Cicely Saunders' point about different styles of worship? Need unity mean uniformity?

8   (a) God draws near to us in his Son and by his Spirit. The apostle Paul rejoices in this – affirming that the Holy Spirit enables us to approach God with confidence, praying (like Jesus) '*Abba*, Father'.

    (b) Paul is also very blunt: 'If anyone does not have the Spirit of Christ he does not belong to Christ' (Rom. 8:9).

Reflect on (a) and (b) in the light of your experience.

9   Read aloud the Harry Williams paragraph (p. 63) and this sentence from the Doctrine Commission of the Church of England: 'The Holy Spirit is the heart-beat of the Christian Church.' Are these high-sounding statements which leave us in the clouds – or do they have practical significance for our lives?

10 John Polkinghorne argues

    (a) that the Holy Spirit is at work in his life in quiet unspectacular ways;

    (b) that the Holy Spirit sometimes can be dramatic and spectacular.

Do you agree? Can you illustrate from personal experience as he and David Hope do on the cassette?

THIRD COURSE

Attending, Exploring, Engaging

SESSION 1: ATTENDING TO GOD

In an interview some years ago, Professor Frances Young – one of the main contributors to the audio-tape which accompanies this course – spoke movingly about her call to become a Methodist minister. She was driving her car when she had what she calls a 'loud thought' telling her to be ordained. She can't remember the journey itself ('I must have been on automatic pilot or something!') but she remembers the experience very clearly. 'I had the whole of my life laid out in front of me; and all its peculiar twists and turns which hadn't seemed to make very much sense suddenly fell into a pattern, as though this was all leading up to that moment and that conclusion. It was quite dramatic in its way.' Frances was ordained as a minister in the Methodist Church on 3 July 1984.

Of course, Frances can't prove to a sceptic that God was guiding her. On such occasions there is always the danger that we think we are attending to God, when we are in fact listening to the deep-down desires (selfish or unselfish) of our own hearts.

I recall a doting mother who was *sure* that God was telling her that her son should break off his engagement to the young woman of whom she disapproved. Unfortunately, God seemed to be telling her son something else! And I remember a devout Christian describing a beautiful house which he had seen in a dream. He took this to mean that he should go ahead with a project for founding a conference centre which (he believed) would flourish in that house. When I last had contact with him the project had not taken off.

This is not to dismiss the possibility that God communicates through dreams, visions and 'loud thoughts'. Certainly there are many examples of this in the Bible. What is more – a great encouragement, this – some of these biblical examples reassure us that God communicates with his people, even when they are not listening very hard. The boy Samuel in bed at night (1 Sam. 3) and the apostle Peter dozing on a rooftop (Acts 10) are two examples. They weren't 'attending to God' at the moment of revelation. What they had in common was a *willingness to listen* and a *desire to be obedient*. Given those two ingredients, I doubt that we can go far wrong.

Some Christians get very hung up on the matter of personal guidance, as they talk about 'God's plan' for their lives. This can be a helpful concept, for it underlines the great truth that God loves each of us personally and individually. But there is no such thing as a doctrine of Christian infallibility. Yes, we have the Scriptures to direct us, God's Son to inspire us, and the Holy Spirit to guide us. But it remains true that 'we all make many mistakes' (Jas. 3:2, RSV).

Imagine that I have made what I now regard as a bad decision. Does this mean that I have lost my way, or strayed from God's plan? Perhaps. If so, does this mean that I must settle for second-best for ever more? No! God's relationship to us is dynamic, not static. In his string quartets, Béla Bartók gives detailed instructions to the instrumentalists and leaves little room for personal interpretation. In contrast, in 'In C' Terry Riley encourages the players to join in the composition. I suspect that God relates to us more like Riley than Bartók. He gives us guidelines – and a lot of space. He is the God of new beginnings. *Wherever* we are in life's maze, he is greater than our circumstances.

The story of our redemption is crucial here. God's saving activity in Christ was necessary because of disobedience. This was 'Plan B' in a big way! But the outcome is wonderful. As St Paul makes clear, we must not sin in order that grace will abound. But grace does abound nonetheless. God does not offer us a blueprint. Instead he offers us himself. And he has no second-best. For 'we know that in all things God works for the good of those who love him' (Rom. 8:28).

This course is accompanied by an audio-tape with fifteen 5-minute 'programmes' (one for each session) featuring:

- **DR DAVID HOPE**, Archbishop of York
- **STEVE CHALKE**, Baptist minister, founder of the Oasis Trust, and television presenter
- **PROFESSOR FRANCES YOUNG** of Birmingham University
- **FATHER GERARD HUGHES**, a Jesuit priest and author of many popular books including *God of Surprises*.

The cassette can be ordered from **York Courses** (for details see p. x).

- **STEVE CHALKE**   God's Spirit speaks to me and guides me, not just by talking to me personally, guiding me personally, but because I am a part of a church and because I am accountable to the church and because we listen to one another . . . So I think, practically, the Holy Spirit overcomes the quirks of my character by working through the body of the church. My mistakes and weaknesses are made up for by other people's strengths and insights.
- **FRANCES YOUNG**   My first-born son has very severe mental and physical disabilities and I found this very difficult to come to terms with. For ten to twelve years I struggled with faith and I remember one moment – I can place it very precisely – in the sitting room at home. As I stood up to do some mundane job in the kitchen it was as though Someone said, 'It doesn't matter to Me whether you believe in Me or not.' Of course, it was only in my head, but it was just mind-blowing.
- **GERARD HUGHES**   One always has to say, 'I am not sure, I think I am doing God's will.' But I recall old Jeremiah saying, 'Oh, how devious is the human heart: perverse too.' Am I really serving God or am I serving myself? We can be extraordinarily subtle in our self-deception. The mark of God's action is peace, tranquillity, strength, joy, and the focus of attention is outwards; it's not on me and my ego.

• **DAVID HOPE**   I have to say that I haven't any experience
at all of a direct communication from God . . . but I don't feel
particularly guilty about it because there is a variety of ways that
God communicates with people in the biblical record. There
are those who seem to have no blinding lights or dramatic
intervention, who faithfully and quietly – sometimes questingly
and questioningly – have just got on with it.

Questions for Groups
Suggested reading: Psalm 25:1–11.
*You may wish to invite members to complete the questionnaire on pp. 175–
7 before tackling the questions.*

1   Has any member of your group had a direct experience of
God like Samuel, St Peter or Frances Young?
2   Read Psalms 10:1 and 13:1. Have you ever longed for God to
communicate with you, directly and immediately, only to find
a deafening silence? What do you make of that? You might
take comfort from the Archbishop of York on the cassette –
and from the end of Psalms 10 and 13.
3   A young Christian says, 'I want to hear what God is saying to
me about my life. How does God communicate with us?'
What would you say?
4   That same young person asks for advice about finding 'God's
plan' for their life. What would you say? And how would you
respond if someone said that because of sin or a bad decision,
they had missed God's plan and made a shipwreck of their
lives?
5   Do you really want to attend to God? Or is that too risky? For
God is in the business of transformation and you might hear
things that you don't want to hear! Draw names out of a hat.
Tell the person whose name you pick whether, in your view,
God wants to 'tame' them or make them more wild and
adventurous in their faith. If that is too embarrassing, each
group member can assess him/herself and share this with the
group.
6   Read Mark 9:7 ('This is my Son, whom I love. Listen to
him'). List one or two things which he might want to say to

you as an individual, as a group, as a church and as an ecumenical group of churches. Are you willing to hear what he has to say?

7   Prayer is about listening to God as well as talking (Steve Chalke). Yet he and Frances Young admit to finding silence difficult. Share any personal experiences which relate to this (you might find it helpful to replay that section on the tape).

8   God gives light to every human being (John 1:9). Yet David Hope maintains that, whatever we share with those of other faiths, God discloses himself fully and uniquely in Jesus Christ. What do you make of that?

9   A bishop at the 1998 Lambeth Conference said that the bishops needed to be together, listening hard for a lengthy period, in order to hear what God is saying to the churches. Is he right? If so, why doesn't God make it easier to hear what he is saying?

10 Gerard Hughes warns against self-deception. How can we guard against using 'God's will' as a cloak for our own wants, wishes and desires?

Notes for Leaders
You may find it helpful to play the tape at the end of your discussion, as well as at the beginning.
At the end, encourage members to ponder whether they have been too talkative or too reticent. If the latter, they may wish to borrow the cassette, listen to Part 2, and jot down one point to bring to the next meeting.
You may wish to close by reading Acts 16:6–10 and saying the Lord's Prayer together.

SESSION 2: ATTENDING TO ONE ANOTHER

'Daddy, Daddy, listen to me, Daddy.' The little boy, tugging at his father's arm with such urgency, understood two things with great clarity. First, the only real evidence of interest in and concern for other people is the attention we give to them. Second, if I do not attend to the other person, I am dismissing him or her as unimportant in my scheme of things. And that was why the little boy protested so persistently. For his father was signalling just how little he seemed to care.

Now I am not accusing that father. No adult can give the kind of total attention which most children would like. But the point made by the little boy is tremendously important. A sign of true humility – and therefore of true greatness in the Christian scheme of things – is a willingness to give undivided attention. I've been fortunate to meet some fine Christians who have affirmed me, simply by paying serious attention to what I've had to say.

Dietrich Bonhoeffer, famous as a German Christian leader who was martyred by the Nazis just before the end of the Second World War, summed this up perceptively in his book *Life Together*:

> The first service that one owes to others in the fellowship consists in listening to them. Just as love for God begins with listening to his Word, so the beginning of love for our friends is learning to listen to them. It is God's love for us that he not only gives us his Word but also lends us his ear. So it is his work that we do for our brothers and sisters when we learn to listen to them . . .
>
> He who can no longer listen to his brother will soon no longer be listening to God either; he will be doing nothing but prattle in the presence of God too. This is the beginning of the death of the spiritual life, and in the end there is nothing left but spiritual chatter arrayed in pious words . . .

There is a kind of listening with half an ear . . . that is only waiting for a chance to speak . . . Christians have forgotten that the ministry of listening has been committed to them by him who is himself the great listener and whose work they share. We should listen with the ears of God that we may speak the Word of God.

Bonhoeffer's words may well be true for most of us, but not for all. For while my temptation is to chatter on, your temptation may be to speak too little. Silence – especially in discussion groups – can be a means of self-defence. For to speak is to risk a rebuttal, or being thought foolish and shallow.

While most of us need to learn to shut up, others need to learn to speak up. In a really supportive group we reach the point where we can think aloud, offering half-thought-through ideas, secure in the knowledge that others will attend carefully and – where necessary – disagree kindly. This is a fine way to sift and refine ideas. Let's pray that God will give us the grace to count others better than ourselves (Phil. 2:3).

There is another important aspect to all this. We are called to attend, not only *to* each but *with* each other. It is as we come together in humility, in fellowship and in prayer that we discern what the Spirit is saying. Archbishop Michael Ramsey spelt out this vital truth: 'It is often in groups of Christians meeting for prayer that a new openness to the Spirit is discovered. It is in such groups that it is vividly realised that the prayer of Christians is not of their own strength or initiative; the Spirit prays within them and they participate in the Spirit's prayer.' Frances Young found deep insights into her personal situation in one such group. Perhaps we will, too.

- **FRANCES YOUNG** The true word that is spoken by someone else, which criticises and which perhaps offers a call – those true words are vitally important for our spiritual health. I think one of the most difficult things in the world is to take criticism constructively, and if we cannot do that then we are not attending.

- **GERARD HUGHES** I think we are extraordinarily defensive. We are afraid really to talk what's in us because of the likely reaction – will we be accepted or rejected? And yet it should be the mark of the Christian Church that we have such trust in God and know ourselves to be accepted and welcomed by God – therefore, why be afraid? But I think the amount of fear around is enormous. It stifles the flow of life.
- **DAVID HOPE** The only way you can begin is by listening . . . You may object hugely to the views of another person but in order to begin to engage with some of that, to begin to unpack it, to understand it, there has to be a meeting. That is the way of the cross; that is the way of Jesus Christ. You have to stick in there, even when the going is at its toughest.
- **STEVE CHALKE** I am always looking for some common ground that we have, that we can begin building a relationship around, and then explore our differences from that point. Jesus approached people outside the Church with compassion, love and generosity. He listened, he had time. What I am after is truth, so if I'm scared of anything that might move me or change me, I'm not going to get far, am I?

Questions for Groups
Suggested reading: Luke 2:41–6.

1   Is Dietrich Bonhoeffer right? Think of two or three people who have affirmed you by attentive listening or hurt you by refusing to listen. Describe them to the group. What can we learn from them? (If your group wants to spend time improving listening skills you might wish to use the Course entitled, 'Please Listen, I'm Shouting', see pp. 209–45.)

2   We sometimes hear the voice of God by attending to other people. That was true for Frances Young. Can you look back to a group meeting, a conversation or even a chance remark, which has significance for your life?

3   Give everyone in the group three minutes to prepare a short statement beginning with one of the following sentences (choose a, b or c):
    (a) I know I talk too much in this group but . . .

(b) I know I ought to say more in this group but . . .

(c) I think I contribute the right amount in this group but . . .

Go round the group asking for the responses. When everyone has had a say, discuss any surprises!

4   You may know people who are greedy for your time and who want to talk and talk and talk. Are we obliged to meet their needs?

5   What do you think about Michael Ramsey's comments on groups (see p. 74)? Does your experience lead you to agree with him?

6   Read Acts 18:23–8. Clearly, there was a lot of good listening going on. What 'yes, buts' might Apollos have been tempted to utter, as he listened to Priscilla and Aquilla?

7   Have you met people whose views you regard as fundamentally wrong – even wicked? Should we listen to, and talk with, them?

8   Our participants have exchanged views with people in other faith communities – Baha'i, Buddhist, Hindu, Jewish, Muslim, etc. Have you had similar experiences? Have these been enriching or frustrating?

9   On a recent ecumenical visit to the Middle East, some participants declined to visit a mosque on grounds of possible 'contamination' – they believe that all other faiths are the works of the devil, designed to direct people away from Jesus Christ. What do you think about this?

10 (a) 'If only' can be a destructive phrase but hard to get out of our minds. Talking can help us deal with the mistakes and 'if onlys' in our lives: e.g. 'If only I hadn't said that/done that', 'If only I'd made a different decision/attended more closely to God'. Group members might be prepared to share their experiences.

    (b) Frances Young encourages us to share our deepest fears/anxieties/hopes but warns against letting our emotions 'hang out' in public. When, where and with whom is deep sharing appropriate?

SESSION 3: EXPLORING OUR FAITH

Remember David Jenkins? It seems ages since you could guarantee that most newspapers would be quoting (or misquoting) chunks from his sermons at the great festivals. For he was Bishop of Durham and tabloid editors had got it into their heads that he didn't actually believe the Christian faith. 'The bishop who doesn't believe' was a gift to be received with thanksgiving.

Some readers will recall a similar furore some thirty years earlier when John Robinson (then Bishop of Woolwich) wrote *Honest to God*. SCM Press printed 7,000 copies of this book, written by an assistant bishop from his sick bed. But *The Observer* gave it a full page under the headline 'Our image of God must go' and the book sold in millions around the world.

These two bishops claimed that they were exploring the faith in which they believed. The press depicted this as the airing of doubts. Whether mistaken or not, John Robinson and David Jenkins sought to be evangelists. They were passionate in their desire to make Christianity credible for modern minds. And both were academics, used to thinking aloud and exploring ideas – following the track wherever it might lead. Their musings disturbed the faith of some, while it strengthened the faith of others. Some believed that they should have been removed from office.

John Habgood – the Archbishop of York who consecrated David Jenkins in York Minster six days before the great fire of 1984 – later reflected with sadness that it is hardly possible for Christian leaders to think aloud in these days of media hype. He seemed to be suggesting that the traditional role of the bishop as a public *guardian of the faith*, must take priority over the role of bishop as *explorer of the faith*. For public musings by senior clerics can too easily be whipped up into a storm by editors wanting to sell newspapers.

It remains true that the Christian faith is rich in experience and ideas. Even without being controversial, there is enough – and more than enough – to explore in the longest lifetime. Given our belief in a 'big' God – a cosmic God, indeed – we should expect our learning and exploring to fill, not just a lifetime, but an eternity too.

The notion of faith as a journey is important to many modern Christians. This inevitably carries with it a degree of provisionality and openness to new insights. But good exploration is best done from a secure base-camp, for no one can be completely open to all possibilities.

To be personal, while I have changed my perspective on a range of issues over the last thirty years, I believe as strongly as ever in the presence of the risen, living Christ, accompanying me through life – challenging, inspiring, comforting, renewing. I've had to open myself to the possibility that this is self-delusion or a psychological prop. I remain as convinced as ever that this is bed-rock reality.

Secure in this great truth, I enjoy exploring the faith. I try to pay careful attention to viewpoints different from my own, and attempt to listen hard before I rush to judgement. Having done that I am not afraid to reject other views, even to say 'nonsense'. Attending to others is quite different from being gullible; we must not be prey to every fashionable idea (2 Tim. 4:1–5). But I am aware that other people are different from me – some very different. Not every Christian wants to probe and search. Many are content simply to accept the views of those with a teaching office within the Church. These, too, are to be honoured as brothers and sisters in Christ, every bit as much as those who seek to push back the frontiers of our understanding.

Christian teachers and preachers have a duty to inform – and to encourage others to think for themselves. But they must discharge this holy calling with sensitivity. For as Cardinal Basil Hume reminded us, it is a serious matter to damage simple faith.*

*Note: The Cardinal made this assertion during a radio interview and I am quoting from memory. He may have used the word 'disturb' (not 'damage'). One group spent fruitful time discussing the difference! You may wish to do the same.

- **DAVID HOPE**   We need to recover a greater sense of simplicity and directness. I think, for example, of the great saints of the north – the Cuthberts and Aidans of this world.

    We need to look again at the Christian doctrine of Creation. There are some very substantial questions here. Is there going to be any world around for our children's children? . . . What is the future if we go on abusing the world as we seem to do in so many areas?

- **FRANCES YOUNG**   We need to understand and affirm our identity. This means listening to people in the past and not thinking we can recreate Christianity now. I am afraid of losing a sense of being open to possibilities . . . we need to take all the richness of the past and carry it forward in creative ways into the future.

- **GERARD HUGHES**   A lot of our ecumenism – although it's made marvellous progress in this century – a lot of it is talk. Do we actually co-operate together in everything? I travel a fair amount in this country; I don't see evidence of that at all.

- **STEVE CHALKE**   The Church will never go out of fashion if it sticks to what Jesus invited us to do and love one another. If you speak to a lot of Christians, especially Christians from my tradition, you wonder why Jesus came for thirty-three years and didn't just make a long weekend of it. Incarnation means getting alongside people, speaking their language, being where they are.

Questions for Groups
Suggested reading: Romans 14:12–23.

1   All ministers make solemn promises at ordination. In this way they declare that they are not 'free agents' – but servants of a community and a tradition to which they owe allegiance. Does this mean that boundaries should be placed around thinking aloud and exploring the faith – in print, in the pulpit, on the radio or TV? Should churches consider setting up a body authorised to give an official stamp of approval and to examine 'dodgy' doctrine?

2   In the article David Jenkins and John Robinson are given as

examples of controversial exploration. You might prefer to suggest different names. If so, who?

3   (a) What do you think of Cardinal Basil Hume's statement that it is a serious matter to damage/disturb simple faith? Can you illustrate this from experience?

     (b) Frances Young responded by saying that there is a fine line between simple faith and superstitious faith. On the other hand (in another setting) David Jenkins said, 'We all live by simple faith' and Sister Lavina Byrne suggested that simple faith is robust faith. What do you think? Can you illustrate any of these points from observation or experience?

     (c) Is Jesus' statement about millstones around necks (Luke 17:1–3) relevant to the previous questions, and if so, how?

4   A minister shared with a group the fact that the Bible nowhere states that Jesus was married or unmarried. From the silence we deduce the latter, but we cannot be certain. This clearly shocked some of his hearers.

     (a) Was that comment foolish or unkind: i.e. did it needlessly disturb simple faith?

     (b) Are we too cautious – staying with the known and accepted – and should we take more risks?

5   Read 1 Corinthians 10:23–11:1. Meat offerings to idols is not an issue for most Western Christians. To which of today's hot issues do the *principles* outlined by St Paul apply?

6   Some Christians argue that God has told today's Church to change the practice of the centuries by (a) ordaining women (b) ordaining practising homosexuals (c) encouraging contraception.

     Does God give different messages to his Church in different centuries, did earlier generations get it wrong, or are modern Christians who argue for these changes wrong? Is John 16:13 relevant here?

7   Most of us have experience of one kind of Christian tradition and spirituality. Do some group members have experience of traditions other than their own, and has this exploration been valuable? Should all Christians seek to broaden their experience

by worshipping in other churches from time to time?

8   Gerard Hughes believes that we need to be bolder in our exploration of ecumenical co-operation, and he asserts that we are better at talking than acting. Do you agree?

9   Gerard Hughes also suggests that there is a good deal of fear to be found within the Church. He asserts that bad ideas should be vanquished by better ideas, not by the heavy hand of authority. Do you have experience of, or opinions about, this?

10 David Hope believes that the Church should explore the doctrine of Creation and its implications for ecology, cloning, medical ethics, etc. Pick one topic in this area for discussion.

SESSION 4: ENGAGING WITH THE WORLD IN SERVICE

'. . . the Church was as concerned with this world as the next: I saw that virtually all of the achievements of Africans seemed to have come about through the missionary work of the Church' (Nelson Mandela in Long Walk to Freedom).

It is fashionable to criticise yesterday's Church for insensitive zeal. No doubt there is much to criticise. For too many Victorians, commerce and Christianity were too closely related. And sometimes there was confusion between the good news of Jesus Christ and the British way of life. But a witness like Nelson Mandela is not easily dismissed. He does not hesitate to criticise the churches – especially (no surprise this) the Dutch Reformed Church. But his praise and gratitude are strongly stated as well.

Coming nearer to home, we have further cause for encouragement. Those of us who are deeply involved in modern church life are well aware of its failings – which are *our* failings. Too often we retreat into the Ark of Church and use it to shelter from the demands of the world. Too often, our concerns are in-house and petty. But we should not sell ourselves short. Professor Robin Gill's research shows that the Christian conscience is still energetic in society. The strong involvement of Christians in a wide range of charitable causes and areas of social need is evidence of this.

Much of this work is unseen and unsung. I was encouraged when I tripped over a pile of shoes in the members' lobby at General Synod. This mountain resulted from an appeal by a member from Leeds who works with homeless people. He invited Synod members to donate good quality, unwanted shoes. I was moved, not by the Synod's generous response, but by the solid year-round work which lay behind the appeal.

Memories are short, and we often forget that many of our leading social action organisations were launched as a result of Christian vision and energy. The Samaritans began as a result of the concern of an Anglican rector in London. Within twenty years, Chad Varah's telephone ministry of listening and befriending had grown into an international movement. Shelter began on 1 December 1966 as the result of the united concern of five housing organisations, the names of three of which contained the word Catholic, Christian or Church. Shelter's first chairman, Bruce Kenrick, was a Christian minister.

Habitat for Humanity is an American Christian initiative which builds subsidised homes for needy people. It has pioneered 'appropriate technology' homes in other continents and countries (Tanzania and Mexico, for example). The hospice movement was started in Britain by Dame Cicely Saunders. She gladly acknowledges that without the inspiration and power of Christ, she would have lacked the strength needed to establish this international movement. Shared Interest is a Christian initiative which works like a building society – but the money on deposit is used to provide seed-corn funding for small businesses in the developing world. Amnesty International was started by Peter Benenson, a Christian lawyer. He developed a team of people who would write to, and about, prisoners of conscience. At a practical level, the existing network of churches was vitally important.

Most modern Christians are comfortable with the image of the Servant Church (even if the image isn't always the reality). But what about that other image – the image of the Warrior Church – which may make us less comfortable? Like it or not, it's there in the Scriptures and in our hymns and songs. 'Soldiers of Christ arise and put your armour on' and 'We are marching in the light of God'. In reality, of course, the soldier of Christ is a key member of the Servant Church. For our fight is with spiritual weapons – the Scriptures, prayer, faith, love. And our struggle is against our personal apathy and against injustice in the world. We do battle with principalities and powers in high places (Eph. 6): a titanic battle indeed. The rest of us thank God for the Salvation Army and the Church Army because their militancy is the militancy of loving service. 'With heart to God and hand to man', as the Salvationist motto puts it. Amen to that, say I.

- **FRANCES YOUNG**   I am absolutely hostile to the notion of Christians disengaging from the world. But sometimes we undervalue the place of the hidden leaven and the contemplative withdrawal, because I think both of those are ways of engaging with the world in a creative but not crusading way. Of course, I do not believe in religious ghettos, because I believe that God is the God of the whole of life.
- **GERARD HUGHES**   There is no use having beautiful liturgical services unless they are a genuine expression of the compassion of God. Hence the prophets' fulminations against empty liturgies. So a church that is not interested in social justice is forced to the Scriptures, because God is the God of justice and reconciliation.
- **DAVID HOPE**   I have in mind the saying of Jesus: 'I have come that they may have life, life in all its fullness.' God sent his Son into the world so that the world might be saved. The world is of God's creating. We have no option but to be involved . . . We have to be where people are.
- **STEVE CHALKE**   I believe the Church should count people in unless they jump out. Let's not throw out the 70 per cent of people in the UK who regard themselves as Christians. Let's say: 'They are standing around in the crowd. They are listening to Jesus.' And let's do all we can to draw them nearer.

Questions for Groups
Suggested reading: Micah 6:6–8.

1 Is there anything on the cassette, or in the text, with which you strongly agree/disagree?
2 Do you have personal experience (as helper or helped) of any of the social action organisations mentioned in the article – or of any other charitable or social action organisations? Is your involvement motivated, in part at least, by your Christian discipleship?
3 Does the notion of the 'Ark of the Church' (i.e. using the Church as a shelter from the storms of life) have a positive part to play in our lives, e.g. retreats? Or is this escapism? Can you illustrate from your own experience?

4   Does your study group, church or group of churches have a vision for the world-wide mission of the Church? Or do you concentrate almost entirely on keeping your own local show 'on the road'? Are you content with the present situation? If not, what practical steps can you take?

5   What might the following images of the Church mean in practical terms for you as a congregation, a study group or a group of churches?
    (a) The Servant Church
    (b) 'Christ's Church militant here in earth' (to quote the Book of Common Prayer)
    (c) The body of Christ

6   Read Ephesians 6:10–20.
    (a) Which of these spiritual weapons do you need to sharpen and strengthen?
    (b) What do you understand by the statement in verse 12 about authorities and powers?

7   A recent survey found that 70 per cent of people in Britain and the USA believe in angels. Do you believe in angels and demons – or are these terms simply a way of speaking about moral and spiritual struggles?

8   Are you surprised/encouraged/challenged by Nelson Mandela's statement on p. 82?

9   Some church leaders speak of the 'Four Ps' of evangelism – Power (from the Holy Spirit); Presence; Persuasion; Proclamation. Does your church have a 'presence' in the community – is it perceived as good news so that it can announce good news, e.g. lunch clubs for the elderly, mother and toddler groups, links with local schools, factories, pubs, etc.?

10 'Preach the Gospel; use words if you must' (St Francis). What is the relationship between a serving church and an evangelising church?

SESSION 5: ENGAGING WITH THE WORLD IN EVANGELISM

To many in the modern Church, the word 'evangelism' has an aggressive, unattractive ring. 'Live and let live,' they say. 'My faith sustains me; what right have I to bother others with it?' But Christianity can never be a privatised religion, and I offer six answers to the question, 'Why evangelise?'

1   *Out of obedience*   The words of the risen Christ to the women on that first Easter morning come down to us across the centuries: 'Go and tell' (Matt. 28:10). This joyful instruction, joyfully obeyed and never rescinded, comes just before the Great Commission: 'Go and make disciples of all nations.' As Christians, we live by the agenda of Another. We have no choice but to obey.

2   *Out of gratitude*   We came to faith because someone passed on the good news to us. If we do not pass it on to others, the 2,000-year-old chain will be broken, for the Church is always one generation from extinction. Out of gratitude to those who told us, encouraged us and inspired us, let us do a bit of telling.

3   *Out of concern for our world*   The connection between evangelism and social action is strong. If the Gospel had not gripped the hearts and minds of key people, then we would have no Samaritans, no Shelter, no Amnesty International, no Leprosy Mission, no Children's Society, no Jubilee 2000, no hospice movement . . .

4   *Out of a desire for freedom*   Evangelism is sometimes depicted as one person forcing unwanted words down someone else's throat. What a travesty! Evangelism thrives in an atmosphere of friendship and love. It is first cousin to education. We are in the business of offering choice, of encouraging people to rethink their lives, of raising horizons, of offering exciting possibilities.

5   ***Out of concern for the truth***   A group of sixth formers opted
     for a leisure course on relaxation. They liked the woman
     who led it and stayed on to talk to her. She gave them details
     of their horoscopes: warning one girl not to marry 'a Pisces',
     telling another that she had a lot of sexual energy. We live in
     a battle of ideas about life – a Babel of voices – some of
     which are dangerous, damaging and exploitative. In the
     middle of all this, the Christian voice must be heard. Jesus
     tells us that we 'do not live by bread alone'. As Christians, it
     is our conviction that the good life is achieved, not by piling
     up riches, but through fellowship, sharing and discipleship.
     We believe that real peace of mind about the future comes
     from faith in the living God, not from horoscopes. If *we*
     don't tell – or better, show – other people these great truths,
     who will?

6   ***Out of love***   We live in a beautiful and exciting world. But it
     is an unpredictable, dangerous and sometimes terrifying world,
     too. Tragic things happen to innocent people and we are forced
     to ask deep questions. Can we *really* find God, truth, meaning
     and love at the centre of our universe? Or are we on our own
     in a cold, uncaring world?

     The good news – the 'glad tidings of great joy' (Luke 2:10)
     – is that God, meaning and truth really are there at the centre
     of our world. The even better news is that they can be at the
     centre of our individual lives, too. The best news of all is that
     this is not wishful thinking. It is based on evidence, on events,
     on widespread experience and, supremely, on a Person. On
     Jesus of Nazareth, whom we worship as Son of God, honour
     as Light and Saviour of the World, and follow as Teacher and
     Lord.

     Take these glorious truths deep into your imagination and
     you will never feel quite the same again, whatever life throws
     at you. For you will have the confidence and reassurance which
     come from being loved, with a love that is sacrificial, practical
     and eternal. Share these glorious truths with someone else in a
     sensitive and appropriate way and you will have performed a
     great act of loving service. Especially to those who 'live lives

of quiet desperation' – and who are 'without hope and without God in the world' (Eph. 2:12).

Euangelio (that we cal gospel) is a greke worde, and sygnyfyth good, mery, glad and joyfull tydings, that maketh a mannes hert glad, and maketh hym synge, daunce and leepe for joye.

William Tyndale (c. 1494–1536)

- **DAVID HOPE** Evangelism means being unselfconscious about your faith and not being afraid to name the name of Jesus Christ, and being able to share your own story with others . . . there have been people who have influenced me greatly and I thank God for them. I think, for example, of a Methodist lay preacher, my maths master.
- **GERARD HUGHES** I was about sixteen and I was praying to win a scholarship exam – I thought prayer would give top-spin to the study! I didn't get the scholarship but somehow prayer had become attractive.
- **STEVE CHALKE** The one thing that all Christians have in common with all non-Christians is this: they hate evangelism! Christians hate doing it and non-Christians hate having it done to them . . . We win people to Christ through *being* good news and win the opportunity to talk about Jesus Christ, our Saviour and their Saviour, too.
- **FRANCES YOUNG** One of the things we need to do is allow ourselves to have our eyes opened and then perhaps to take every opportunity we can to allow others to have their eyes unveiled so that they too can see the presence of God. Maybe we need to have a little bit more courage to tell the story and affirm our identity, even though affirming our identity can sometimes be mistaken by other people.

  I think I would want to characterise the major turning point back to faith as a return to my roots. Both my grandfathers were Methodist ministers and my parents were both Methodist local preachers for whom Christian commitment in the whole of life was of fundamental importance.

Questions for Groups
Suggested reading: Matthew 28:16–20.

1 Look back down the years. How did you come to faith in Christ?

   (a) Can you pick out a significant event, organisation, experience and/or person?

   (b) As you reflect on this, what do you learn about evangelism?

2 Discuss the following statements:

   – 'Evangelism means one beggar showing another beggar where he found bread' (D.T. Niles).

   – 'Evangelism means carrying Jesus in your heart and giving the presence of Jesus to someone else' (attributed to Mother Teresa).

   – 'My friend is rather shy but she formed a bridge and Jesus Christ walked over it.'

   – 'Evangelism is helping people to belong so that they can believe' (Bishop John Finney).

3 Many people see evangelism as a 'corporate' activity. 'Belonging precedes believing' is how Professor Robin Gill puts it. So a most effective evangelistic strategy is for a Christian to say to a friend, neighbour or family member: 'I'm going, it's going to be good, will you come with me?' Draw up two lists of (a) events, activities or services in your church to which you might invite people, and (b) people whom you might invite.

4 (a) What is your personal response to the word 'evangelism'?

   (b) Do you believe that the Great Commission (Matt. 28:19–20) applies to you? If so, what might this mean in practical terms?

5 We live with a Babel of ideas, each battling for allegiance of mind and soul. Do you agree? Which voices speak loudest today? How can the Christian voice be heard in the modern market-place, and what should it be saying?

6 Frances Young suggested that some churches are God-centred

and prayerful but dying nonetheless. What do you think about that?

7   Contrary to many reports, the world Church is growing numerically and so are many Western churches.
    (a) Is your church growing or declining?
    (b) What are its weak points? How can these be strengthened?
    (c) What are its strong points? How can these be strengthened further?

8   Steve Chalke asserts that growing churches are characterised by laughter.
    (a) What do you think about that?
    (b) Which other features are likely to be significant for growth? (See p. 140.)

9   A Buddhist says, 'You Christians talk about the Gospel, the good news. What is this good news?' How would you respond?

10 Discuss what happens next in your group: e.g. disband, throw a party, meet for another group course in a few weeks. Or you might consider arranging an evangelistic supper party, inviting friends/family/neighbours and a visiting speaker with an interesting life story which illustrates the meaning of faith.

You may wish to close by reading one of the Summaries on pp. 24 and 129 (using various voices).

'Churches do not grow numerically by trying to get *bigger* but by trying to get *better*' (Dr Steven Croft). Canon Robert Warren's *Characteristics of Healthy Churches* is available from York Courses (see page x). *The National Church Development Handbook* by Christian A. Schwarz (BCGA) is also relevant.

FOURTH COURSE

Live Your Faith

PRACTICAL ARRANGEMENTS:
SUGGESTIONS FOR WEEK ONE

- Welcome members with coffee and conversation (or just conversation, with coffee afterwards).
- People introduce themselves or play a mixing game (e.g. pair up with someone you don't know and give a personal introduction for two minutes each; then link with another pair and introduce each other). *Or* ask partners to describe an early childhood memory.
- Give out pen and paper to each group member.
- Possibly give out Bibles or Gospels to each group member.
- Play the audio-tape. Ask group members to jot down any points they wish to discuss, as they listen – points with which they strongly agree or disagree, or points they want clarified. Discuss these.
- Tackle some of the questions or projects in the first chapter.

Note: This course was originally published as a booklet by CPAS. I am extremely grateful for their permission to include it in this book.

The audio-tape which accompanies this course is likely to become a collectors' item, for it contains the voices of several fine Christians who have died within the last few years.
- **DR DONALD ENGLISH**, an outstanding broadcaster and preacher. Donald was Chair of the World Methodist Council and President (twice) of the Methodist Conference.

- **LORD TONYPANDY**, whose voice was recognised by millions when he uttered the words, 'Order, Order'. As George Thomas he was Speaker of the House of Commons. He was also a Methodist local preacher.
- **ROY CASTLE** was a well-loved TV personality, who became famous for his heroic struggle with lung cancer.
- **FIONA CASTLE**, Roy's widow, is still very much alive! Fiona is well known – and well loved – for her books and speaking ministry.

The cassette may be ordered from York Courses (see p. x).

SESSION 1: THE KEY

> Let us fix our eyes on Jesus, the author and perfecter of our faith. (Heb. 12:2)

In this famous verse, the writer of the letter to the Hebrews compares the Christian life to a race. It is not a sprint but a long-distance haul; we are to run with 'persistence' or 'perseverance'. In the Barcelona Olympics, the marathon runners found

- **obstacles** – the road was twisty and there were some very steep hills;
- **refreshments** – tables with refreshing drinks.

The Christian life is like this. We face trials and temptations. It is no picnic. But it includes times of joy and encouragement.

There are *two key differences* between the Christian race and an Olympic marathon:

1 ***We are not in a competition***   Gold medals are not rationed in our race – a special prize is minted for *every single person* who finishes the course (2 Tim. 4:7, 8).
2 ***We are given help***   The marathon rules are clear: *no outside help* is allowed. You are on your own. Get a bit of help from anyone else and you are disqualified. In contrast, the Christian race is all about giving and receiving help.

Our main assistance is the presence of a Pacemaker. Jesus has run this race before us and he runs with us now. He challenges us when we are lazy but he refreshes us when we are weary. He will even carry us from time to time. *He* is the key to the Christian life, says the writer of Hebrews. 'Let us fix our eyes on Jesus . . .' One important way of doing this is to read the Gospels in the New

Testament. When we do so, we find that Jesus is . . .

- *Our Teacher* If we want to learn about God, about faith, about life and about ourselves, we shall study his words and his approach to life.
- *Our Lord* We can read the words of a great teacher, say 'how interesting' and leave it there. But if we are serious about following Jesus, we shall say, 'With God's help, I will put this into practice.'
- *Our Saviour* The teaching of Jesus is sometimes tough and challenging. His standards are very demanding. But he is gentle and understanding too. The Gospels are full of stories in which Jesus forgave and encouraged moral and spiritual failures – and pointed them to better things. So we can come with confidence, asking for forgiveness, strength and inspiration.

Is It All Made Up?

Modern writers sometimes hit the headlines (and make a lot of money) by claiming that Jesus did not exist – or that the story has been distorted. They argue that the Gospel accounts were invented or greatly exaggerated by the early Church. This position is shot through with problems, as the following story suggests.

In 1912, the Cambridge mathematician G. H. Hardy 'discovered' a brilliant Indian mathematician called Ramanujan. It happened like this . . .

Ramanujan – an Indian clerk with little education – wrote a long letter to Hardy which was full of complicated mathematical formulae. This posed a puzzle for Hardy: was the letter a hoax or was it the genuine article? Hardy soon realised that even his cleverest student could not have invented the letter; the mathematics was far too advanced and original. He remarked: 'I have never seen anything in the least like them before. A single look at them is enough to show that they could only be written down by a mathematician of the highest class . . . they must be true because, if they were not true, no one would have the imagination to invent them.'

It seems to me that the same can be said of much of the material in the New Testament – and especially those claims made for and by Jesus. They simply must be true, because no one would have had the imagination to invent them – least of all *Jewish* men and women, to whom they would have been so shocking. You would need someone of the stature of Jesus to invent the teaching of Jesus.

The Greatness of Jesus

The New Testament makes it clear that Jesus was a real human being. Like us he had emotional 'highs' and 'lows'. Like us he got weary, hungry, thirsty and tired. But that same New Testament makes it clear that Jesus is unique. Even exalted titles like Prophet and Messiah aren't big enough to contain him. The writers were forced to squeeze language to its limits with phrases like Lord, Redeemer, Son of God and Light of the world.

> When we talk about believing in Jesus, there is a content to it. It's not believing that here was once a nice man who did good things, and who better for an example? That's very thin indeed in terms of New Testament interpretation. It's a person about whom they say: Son of Man, Lord, Saviour, Emmanuel, Word of Life. And every one of those ways of describing him is throbbing with meaning. (Dr Donald English)

Ideas for Groups

I have provided plenty of questions to cater for different kinds of groups. But this is not an obstacle course! Please select those questions or practical activities which suit your situation. If you only manage one or two, that's fine. Or you may prefer to draw up your own questions, perhaps as a group exercise. Some of the activities are intended for groups which prefer 'doing' to 'talking'. You may wish to spread each session over two or more weeks.

Quiz Time – What do you know?

Note to group leaders: Allow a few minutes for people to fill this in. Before doing so, reassure the group that no one will be asked directly for his/her answer and no one else will know what they have written, unless they are happy about this. When time for filling in the answers is up, go through the list, encouraging people to call out if they know the answer.

1   Jesus lived in the country today called . . . .
    (Egypt, Jordan, Israel)
2   At home, Jesus learned the trade of . . . .
    (fishing, carpentry, teaching)
3   Jesus' mother was called . . . .
    (Mary, Martha, Elizabeth)
4   One man prepared the way for Jesus . . . .
    (James, Thomas, John)
5   Jesus was too good to be tempted . . . . (True or false?)
6   Jesus once called a disciple 'Satan'. Who was he? . . . .
    (James, John, Peter)
7   Jesus called a group of . . . .
    special disciples (10, 11, 12)
8   One of these betrayed him . . . . (Levi, Judas, Peter)
9   Jesus' disciples were all scholarly people . . . .
    (True or false?)
10 Jesus knew everything . . . . (True or false?)
11 Jesus was never anxious or afraid . . . .
    (True or false?)
12 Jesus understands what we are going through . . . .
    (True or false?)

Discuss your answers and pick out anything which is particularly interesting or significant

Bible references:
1	Luke 2:32	2	Matt. 13:55	3	Mark 6:3
4	Mark 1:6–8	5	Luke 4:1–13	6	Mark 8:27–33
7	Luke 6:12,13	8	Luke 6:16	9	Acts 4:13
10	Mark 13:32	11	Mark 14:32–6	12	Hebrews 4:15,16

For Discussion

1 People sometimes talk of 'a personal relationship with Jesus'

- What do you understand by this?
- Can you illustrate this from your own experience or from the experience of others?

2 Group members are invited to explain the circumstances in which they began their own journey of discipleship.

3 (a) Can you think of an example from your own life or someone else's when you were:
  - challenged by Jesus as Teacher and Lord?
  - encouraged by Jesus as Teacher and Saviour?

  (b) Or, for you, is Jesus a rather remote figure in history, who has little relevance to daily life?

  (c) Share your opinions and insights, trying hard to 'enter into' someone else's different understanding and experience.

4 We have thought of three titles for Jesus: Teacher, Lord and Saviour. What are the implications of each title for us today?

5 There are many more titles in the New Testament.
  (a) Brainstorm your group to draw up a list of these.
  (b) Turn to St John's Gospel and go through quickly, looking for titles for Jesus (Gospels or Bibles need to be provided).
  (c) What do these titles mean for our lives today?

6 Jesus said some remarkable things. Read them and ask: did he intend us to take him literally, or was he pointing us in a certain direction? Group members are asked to describe (or imagine) concrete situations in their own lives, or other people's, where these words have (or might) hit home.

- Turn the other cheek
- Sell your possessions and give to the poor
- If anyone comes after me, he must hate his father and his mother
- Forgive seventy times seven
- Take no anxious thought for tomorrow

7   Read the words of Albert Schweitzer (p. 99). Does your experience of life and the living Christ resonate with his?
8   If you were devising questions or activities on the great theme of 'Jesus as the key to life', what would you add?

For Action

1   Consider the theme 'Jesus and the Outcast'. First read Luke 19:1–10 and John 8:1–11. Then attempt to act out these episodes. Finally, by means of role play, put the same theme into a modern setting. (Who are today's outcasts? What is Jesus' attitude to them? What is he saying to us?)
2   You may prefer to explore the theme by means of painting, a group collage, a banner . . .
3   Work out one or two pieces of practical service that you can offer
     –   shopping for, or visiting, the elderly
     –   writing letters to prisoners of conscience
     –   delivering parish magazines
     –   tending the church grounds
     Extend this list and sort out priorities.
4   Some churches display an Easter Garden with the empty tomb or a Nativity scene at Christmas. Plan one or both of these – or something similar based on another episode from the New Testament (Pentecost perhaps?). Decide who will bring or make what and where you hope it will be displayed. Diplomacy is required! Check first that this isn't being prepared by another group of church members.
5   By now you will gather that I am struggling hard with a good idea! Just how can we use our practical skills – as individuals and as a group – to explore what it means to follow Jesus today? Share your ideas.

To Close Your Time Together

Read Luke 24:13–19. Then read aloud these words of Albert Schweitzer. After this sit quietly, then end the meeting with the Lord's Prayer, or a time of open prayer, or silence, or a song, or whatever suits your group.

> He comes to us as one unknown, without a name, as of old by the lakeside he came to those men who knew him not. He speaks to us the same word: 'Follow me', and sets us to the tasks which he has to fulfil for our time. He commands. And to those who obey him, whether they be wise or simple, he will reveal himself in the toils, the conflicts, the sufferings which they shall pass through in his fellowship, and . . . they shall learn in their own experience who he is. (Albert Schweitzer)

SESSION 2: PRAYER

Prayer is a universal activity. In every age and in every culture, men and women instinctively cry out to that great 'force' or 'power' which they perceive to be behind the mystery of life.

Perhaps surprisingly, this instinct remains strong even at the turn of the third millennium. The word 'secular' is sometimes used to describe our age. But we could equally well use words like 'superstitious' and 'spiritual'. Horoscopes abound, and surveys suggest that in modern Britain about 70 per cent believe in God (and in angels), and more than 60 per cent of people pray from time to time – compared with around 10 per cent who attend church.

The most universal prayer consists of one word: 'Help'. There are many examples of this desperate cry meeting with an apparent answer. Here is one: 'I was trapped in a freezer and I knew that if God didn't send someone to free me I'd die. I prayed and I was released. It started me thinking.'

This prayer left that man with a problem. Was his escape a coincidence, or was it a genuine answer to prayer? That question set him on the path to Christian faith and discipleship, and this in turn involved him in a life-long exploration of the marvels and mysteries of prayer. For, clearly, there is much more to prayer than an occasional cry for help.

It might *start* there, but that is simply a gateway. This is not to say that Christian prayer has to be complicated. Like so much else in the Christian faith, it is based on a *relationship* – our relationship with God and with our fellow believers. We are children of God with numerous brothers and sisters, who pray with us and for us.

Prayer is a matter of *being with God*. Of course, we are in his presence all the time. 'For in him we live and move and have our being' as the apostle Paul put it in Acts 17:28. But prayer involves putting ourselves *consciously* into the presence of God. We can do this anywhere and at any time: walking, driving, standing at a bus stop . . . But most Christians find that it helps to *make* a time each day to be quiet and still. I stress 'make' because this doesn't come easily in the rush of daily life.

Prayer has many aspects. Michael Ramsey – Archbishop of York before he became the hundredth Archbishop of Canterbury – put it like this.

> *Adoration* means being with God – *humble*
> *Confession* means being with God – *sorrowful*
> *Thanksgiving* means being with God – *grateful*
> *Supplication* means being with God – *needful*
> *Listening* means being with God – *attentive*.

The first four forms of prayer listed above are often summed up in a useful codeword: ACTS.

Each kind of prayer can be engaged in individually or in the company of others. They can be adapted to suit all circumstances and all personalities. Some prefer to pray in deep silence; others like to pray with other people in exuberant joy. All these are valid variations, provided they are rooted in a deepening relationship with the living God.

Christians do not pray to an impersonal force or power. We pray to 'the God and Father of our Lord Jesus Christ' (Eph. 1:3). One of Jesus' great gifts to us is his favourite prayer word: '*Abba*'. It is an Aramaic word meaning 'Daddy'. It breathes trust and intimacy – the basis and goal of all Christian prayer.

Chris's Story

Chris had no church background and wasn't sure whether she believed in God or not. She was married with two young children when life began to fall apart. Her husband went to live abroad and she moved into a council house with her parents and brother. She was so desperate that she considered suicide – family suicide, as she couldn't bear to leave her children behind.

In desperation she prayed, 'If you are there – please help me.' Within a few weeks life had taken a U-turn for the better and she had moved into a house of her own. Then she faced another problem: was this an answer to prayer or a coincidence? Chris began to attend her local church and spent a year watching, listening and pondering before taking her first step into Christian discipleship. Her life continues to have ups and downs, with unexpected twists and turns. But her faith in Jesus as the key to life remains strong.

Ideas for Groups
For Discussion

1   Have any group members experienced dramatic answers to prayer, like the man trapped in a freezer or Chris's house purchase?

Do you expect definite answers to your prayers?

2   Read Mark 14:36 and 2 Corinthians 12:7–10. In these passages we find two of history's most famous prayers answered with a firm 'NO'. Christians sometimes say that every prayer is answered – but that the answer can be 'No' or 'Wait' as well as 'Yes'. Is this just a cop-out from the uncomfortable fact that our prayers sometimes seem to go unanswered?

3   Do you feel that Questions 1 or 2 place the emphasis in the wrong place? i.e. should we be less concerned with answers than with building our relationship with God?

4   Ask experienced 'pray-ers' in the group to share their own prayer discipline, and their thoughts about:

- Daily prayer
- Arrow prayers
- Chatting prayers
- Formal prayers
- Free-wheeling prayers
- Written prayers

- Open prayer
- Silent prayer

5   Muslims and Hindus pray in an open and unembarrassed way
     at home and in public. Why are we Christians embarrassed
     about praying except in a worship service? Can we/should we
     attempt to reverse this trend? How? Would saying Grace at
     meals be a helpful step forward?
6   Read Ephesians 5:19–20, 6:18–20 and Luke 18:1–8, 18:9–14.
     Discuss the teaching on prayer in these passages.
7   If *you* were devising questions or activities on prayer, what
     would you add to this list?
8   Do you agree that our age is secular, superstitious and spiritual?

For Action

1   Have you ever experienced a 'retreat' – a time (from half a day
     to thirty days) dedicated to being with God in quiet reflection
     and prayer? If 'yes' – describe your experience. If 'no' – why
     not try it?
2   *Learning to pray*
     British people are often embarrassed at the prospect of pray-
     ing publicly except in a 'proper' service of worship. Great
     sensitivity is needed to help new Christians to develop
     confidence in prayer as a natural activity for believers meeting
     in a group.
         Give out pieces of paper. Each member writes down a one-
     sentence 'thank you' prayer. The leader takes these in, shuffles
     them and redistributes. The leader begins by reading out loud
     the prayer on his/her paper. 'Amen' is the signal for the next
     person to read. Continue round the circle. This can be repeated
     for 'request' prayers. In following weeks, people may be ready
     to do this without writing first. At first this exercise should
     take no longer than about five minutes.
3   *Prayer visiting*
     Don't be put off by the title. This is not about praying with
     people on their doorstep! It is about discovering prayer needs.
     This scheme is based on the fact that the majority of people

believe in God and that many non-churchgoers are secret 'pray-ers' who value the prayers of others.

First deliver a letter (example below) which sensitively asks for prayer requests. Follow this up within a few days, by going out in pairs as part of a group exercise. Ideally, this will be done ecumenically, by churches working together.

Meet for prayer before and after visiting. Aim for each pair to visit about twenty homes – unless an in-depth conversation opens up. Don't rush; it's *people* that matter. Note names and addresses of people who show interest and hand these, plus requests for prayer, to your organiser.

Many churches have used this scheme and several have been warmly received by non-churchgoers.

Dear Friend,

This letter comes from the members of St Mary's (RC), New Lane Methodist and St Agatha's (C.of E.). We are keen to be of service to all people in our area, whether or not they attend church. As Christians, we believe in the power of prayer. In our experience it releases God's love into our world and into our lives. Because of this, we shall be praying for all who live in your road next Sunday.

You may have particular needs which you would like us to pray about. Perhaps someone in your family is ill; maybe you are facing a difficult decision or finding life hard at present; maybe you want to give thanks for something special.

In a few days' time, two church members will call on you. We shall wear official badges so you can be sure we are genuinely from the churches. If you have any items for prayer, we will be glad to hear from you.

Of course, you may not share our faith in God and prayer. Or you may not want to share personal matters with strangers. If so, we won't stay longer than it takes you to say 'thank you', or 'get lost'.

You may also like to join us in Sunday worship when we pray for the needs of the area. We should love to welcome you. Our main Sunday services are held at 10.30 a.m. and 6.30 p.m. There are creche facilities, and we can give you details of Sunday schools and mid-week activities.

But even if you don't come, we shall still be praying for you. With warmest good wishes,

To End Your Time Together
Read Luke 11:9–13, then read this statement by Cardinal Basil Hume. Spend a few moments in silence, pondering the question, 'Where am I in relation to this?'

Holiness involves friendship with God. God's love for us and ours for him grows like any relationship with other people. There comes a moment, which we can never quite locate or catch, when an acquaintance becomes a friend. In a sense, the change from one to the other has been taking place over a period of time, but there comes a point when we know we can trust the other, exchange confidences, keep each other's secrets. We are friends. There has to be a moment like that in our relationship with God. He ceases to be just a Sunday acquaintance and becomes a weekday friend. (*To be a Pilgrim*: SPCK)

Finally, invite one member of your group to say a closing prayer.

SESSION 3: THE COMMUNITY

Sally and Bill grew up outside the Church. But they were interested in Christianity, and when a friend invited them to a Christian meeting they were glad to attend. What they heard made sense and they decided that they wanted to accept Jesus as their Teacher and Saviour and obey him as their Lord. But they couldn't understand why they needed to attend church to do this. Why couldn't they be loyal disciples without all that . . . ?

Yes, Sally and Bill are an imaginary couple. Or are they? There are many Sallys and Bills around, and I hope, before reading on, you will try to work out what *you* would say to them. (As it is tempting to see how someone else answers a difficult question, the next two paragraphs are printed upside down.)

My answer would go something like this.

1   *A spiritual hospital*   From personal experience I understand Sally's and Bill's problem. The Church can be a pretty crumby outfit and when people accuse it of hypocrisy and draw attention to its failings, we know that what they say has real bite.

Perhaps we shouldn't expect anything else. Christians are people who admit that they are moral and spiritual failures. That is why we confess our sins and acknowledge our need of Jesus as Saviour. The Church isn't a health farm – it's more like a spiritual hospital. And you don't go to hospital to show how fit you are. One church has a large notice outside which declares, 'This church is for sinners only'. That sums it up. If you are a moral and spiritual failure – welcome to the Church!

2   *The Church is people*   The picture of failure is true but incomplete. From personal experience I know that the Church rings true in many ways. There is a lot of love and support around.

Without encouragement from Christian friends and teaching from Christian leaders, my faith would soon go off the boil. At the beginning of his ministry, Jesus chose a *group*. Ever since, it has thrived on *friendship*. We need one another.

An old Scot began to miss church on Sundays. One winter evening his minister called. Both were men of few words and they sat by the fire in silence. At length the minister picked up the tongs, took a red-hot coal from the fire and put it on the hearth. It went black and became cool. He replaced it among the other coals and it became red again. The story has a happy ending. The old Scot got the point. He was in church next Sunday.

---

3   *The Church provides opportunities*   The Church has a much better track record than many people realise. Several of our great caring movements have Christian roots, even though they are not limited to Christians in their membership. The **Samaritans** were started by a London vicar. **Shelter** began with significant Christian input. **Amnesty International** started as a result of the vision and prayer of one Christian man and needed a network of churches to get established. **The hospice movement** – launched by believers – goes from strength to strength. Mailings continue to flop on to my door mat from Christian organisations working among the homeless, the hungry, among refugees and leprosy sufferers . . .

Belonging to the Church means that we are part of a network which can get things done. The Church can channel our desire to help. For example, Christian Aid week raises millions of pounds for the developing world, by the united efforts of the churches. We can do *together* what we cannot do *apart*.

4   *The Church enables us to worship*   We can pray on our own but we need other people if we are to worship. Singing hymns in the bath is one thing; singing hymns with 10 or

100 or 1,000 other people is quite another!

Worship lifts our hearts and our horizons. The word 'eucharist' means thanksgiving. The Church is the community of the grateful. In our imagination we come together with other like-minded people and kneel humbly at the foot of the cross, acknowledging our needs and expressing our gratitude.

Worship isn't escapism. It opens us up to the love of God and releases that love into a needy world. Church services often end with a prayer like this: 'Send us out into the world in the power of your Spirit to love and serve . . .'

There was once a man who had three nasty big boils, and he went to the doctor and asked for each of them to be treated or removed. And the doctor said, 'I can do nothing perm-anent with those boils unless we get rid of the poison in your system which is causing them.' So, too, the human race, very sick and having terrible boils in the social and moral order, wants to be rid of them, because it would be happier without them. But this human race does not grasp that the trouble is a poison in the system, and the sickness is that of a deep derangement in the relation of mankind to the Creator.

Go to the root. 'Do justly, love mercy, walk humbly with thy God,' said the prophet. Far and wide, men and women try fitfully to do the first and the second, and push aside the third. So justice is blind, and mercy too often calculating and patronising. The root is the right relation of man to Creator: and when Christians are concerned about what they call worship they are concerned, not with something remote or escapist, but with the root of the world's predicament. (Archbishop Michael Ramsey, hundredth Archbishop of Canterbury)

Ideas for Groups
For Discussion
1   What would *you* say to Sally and Bill?

2   Read and discuss the following assertion by Archbishop George Carey: 'It is impossible to be a Robinson Crusoe Christian. We need the human family in order to live and grow and similarly we need the Christian family to grow up as Christians.'

3   The New Testament acknowledges three realities about the Church. First we see a group of well-meaning but ordinary people. They squabble and sulk and feel jealous of one another. But for all their faults they are very effective. They get things done. Indeed, they turn the world upside down.

    The New Testament goes on to describe the Church in ideal, eternal terms. It gives us a glimpse of those ordinary people as God sees them, with all their raw potential fulfilled. The Bible does this through a series of lovely word pictures. You are invited to look up these references, discover the word pictures and discuss what they might mean for us today: Matthew 5:13–16; Luke 12:32; Acts 9:2; 1 Corinthians 12:27; 1 Peter 2:4–12; Revelation 7:9.

4   Michael Ramsey suggests that worship is a channel through which God's love flows into the world. As a young man, Thomas Merton (who later became a Roman Catholic Trappist monk) saw men at prayer and wrote: 'This is the center of America. I had wondered what was keeping the country together, what has been keeping the universe from cracking in pieces and falling apart. It is places like this monastery.'

    Do you feel the thrill and force of this way of looking at worship and prayer – or do you think it is exaggerated?

5   If you were challenged to explain how worship in church connects with 'real life', what would you say?

6   Consider the following parable. You have a dream in which you see a building on fire. You rush to the scene and find six buckets of water. You look behind you and see six sleeping firemen. You wake up wrestling with the question: 'Which way shall I throw the water?'

    Does this have an application to the modern Church in the light of Ephesians 5:13–17?

7   If you were devising questions or activities on the Church,
    what would you add?

For Action

1   Devise a collage, picture or banner based on the word pictures
    for the Church in Question 3 above. This can be done
    individually or as a group.
2   Do the same for word pictures about the individual Christian
    after filling in the table below.

Reference	Description	Meaning
Matthew 5:13	Salt	Active in society
Matthew 5:14	Light	Reflecting Christ's light
John 13:34,35	. . . .	Following and learning from Jesus
Acts 1:8	. . . .	. . . .
Acts 5:14	Believer	. . . .
Acts 11:26	Christian	Our lives are based on Christ
1 Corinthians 6:19	. . . . .	God lives in us, by his Spirit
Ephesians 1:1	. . . .	. . . .
2 Timothy 2:3	. . . .	We fight against evil – in the world and in ourselves.
Philemon 16	Brother	. . . .
1 Peter 2:11	Refugee, alien, stranger or pilgrim	. . . .

3   Consider this question: how can your church reach out into
    your locality with the good news of God's love revealed in
    Jesus? (CPAS has produced several A4 photocopyable books
    on evangelism. See p. ii.)
4   To support your efforts to reach out you might consider
    praying for your locality by means of a 'prayer walk'.

    • Meet with others in a house or church hall.
    • Pray together and decide which roads you intend to visit.
    • Walk down those roads in twos or threes, praying for the
      people and institutions (schools, pubs, factories).

- Prayer need not be open and obvious – but it can be. Some groups prefer to go after dark!

5   You could pray for your town, city, village or locality in the security of the church hall using slides, if walking daunts you.

For All

Ask various members of your group to read aloud different sections from the Summaries on pp. 24 and 129. Sit quietly and take this in, then say together the following prayer.

Almighty God, who called your Church to witness that you were in Christ reconciling the world to yourself: help us so to proclaim the good news of your love, that all who hear it may be reconciled to you; through him who died for us and rose again and reigns with you and the Holy Spirit, one God, now and for ever. Amen.

SESSION 4: THE BIBLE

Men turn this way and that in their search for new sources of comfort and inspiration, but the enduring truths are to be found in the Word of God. (Queen Elizabeth the Queen Mother)

It's really a journey through life. It makes sense of the universe we find ourselves in. The story line is tremendous. I think people forget what a good tale it tells – the story of the Children of Israel is the greatest story ever written anyway; and then [with] the coming of Jesus you have a whole new song being sung. So once you get into it, you find that it holds together . . . But also it's so diverse . . . It's like having a great compendium of friends. It just is the greatest document of the lot, and once you've read it, your life is never the same. (Popular broadcaster Brian Redhead)

We live in a confusing world with many different opinions and ideas on offer. Can we find reliable guidance? If so, where? In answer to these questions, Christians speak of

- guidance from God's Spirit – the Holy Spirit
- guidance from God's Word – the Bible.

Neither is given to us on a plate. We have to work at 'listening' to the voice of God's Spirit in quietness, humility and obedience. And we have to work hard as we seek to apply wisdom from the ancient Scriptures to life in the modern world.

We have no guarantee that we won't make mistakes. Indeed, the Bible itself assures us that we will (Jas. 3:2)! But as God's Spirit within us throws light upon God's Word in front of us, we discover the will of God for our lives and for our world. For this reason, many Christians read a Bible passage each day and various organisations publish notes to help them (e.g. Bible Reading Fellowship, International Bible Reading Association, Scripture Union, *Every Day with Jesus*, church lectionaries).

But Bible reading isn't just a solitary activity. We can learn a lot *together*. One reason for attending church is to hear God's Word explained and applied in the sermon. And many Christians find considerable help from Bible study in a house group.

Ancient Book – Modern World

People sometimes think of the Bible as presenting more questions than answers. Questions like:

- How can an old book shed light on life in the modern world?
- Are the accounts of Jesus' life reliable?
- How are we to understand Adam and Eve in a scientific age?
- What about the violent bits?

These are important issues which call for careful consideration, in a spirit of open enquiry. I have attempted to face these questions in *The Case Against Christ* and *Teach Yourself Christianity* (Hodder & Stoughton). But it would be wrong to see the Bible mainly as 'a problem'. Rather, let us rejoice in the Holy Scriptures, which are still the world's number one best-seller, and which continue to convey vital and life-giving truth to a needy world.

John's Story

At sixty John took early retirement from the hospital service in York. He had worked in Supplies. Instead of watching the world from his armchair, he believed that God was calling him to use his expertise overseas. So he linked up with a charity which ensures that hospital supplies reach the point of need in developing countries. In no time at all he found himself in Afghanistan, where he got more than he bargained for.

John found himself in the middle of a war. For three weeks he was the only English-speaking person in his area of Kabul. He spent many hours flat on his face hoping that neither a stray shell nor a bullet would find him. Each day he read his Bible. One particularly difficult morning his Bible fell open at Psalm 116 and he read these words: 'For you, O LORD, have delivered my soul from death, my eyes from tears, my feet from stumbling, that I may walk before the Lord in the land of the living' (vv. 8, 9).

The whole Psalm breathes faith in God's protection and gave John courage, hope and faith. He returned home safely but is still refusing to view the world from his armchair!

Ideas for Groups
Quiz Time

1   The Old Testament was written in . . . .
    (Hebrew, Greek, Latin)
2   The New Testament was written in . . . .
    (Hebrew, Greek, Latin)
3   The OT is longer than the NT . . . . (True or false?)
4   The NT writer who wrote most is . . . . (Paul, Luke, John)
5   List the four Gospel writers . . . .
6   The OT took about . . . . years to write
    (50, 200, 1,000 years)
7   The NT took about . . . . years to write
    (50, 200, 1,000 years)
8   The OT contains . . . . books (27, 39, 42)
9   The NT contains . . . . books (27, 39, 42)
10 The most famous Bible verse is . . . .

Answers

1 Hebrew 2 Greek 3 True 4 Luke (he wrote Luke's Gospel and Acts) 5 Matthew, Mark, Luke, John 6 1,000 years 7 50 years 8 39 9 27 10 Who knows? I guess Psalm 23:1 or John 3:16.

For Discussion

1   You are to be shipwrecked on that legendary desert island. But instead of eight records, you are allowed to take:
    (a) one piece of music
    (b) two books
    (c) five passages from the Bible.
    Which would you choose? (You can distribute Bibles to help this go with a swing, if you wish.)

2   Imagine that you are visiting someone who is extremely ill, though very alert. A Bible is lying by the bedside and they ask you to read from it. Which passages would you choose?

3   More experienced members of your group are invited to explain:

    • What the Bible means to them
    • How they read the Bible

    Other members of the group are invited to make comments and ask questions.

4   People in Bible times could travel no faster than horses or camels could carry them. We can travel by jet. Yet we have a great deal in common with those ancient people and it is these common factors with which the Bible is concerned e.g. we still experience fear, fall in love and . . .
    (a) Draw up a list of factors which separate us from people in Bible times.
    (b) Draw up a list of factors which link us with people in Bible times.

5   Read Luke 18:9–14. In the light of this parable, what do you think Ephesians 2:8–10 means?

6   A recent Bible Society survey showed that 66 per cent of churchgoers had not read the Bible during the previous week and only 15 per cent read it every day. What do you think about this?

For Action

1   Dramatise some Bible passages (i.e. dividing the text between several voices) to help you 'get into' the story and the action.

2   Using role play, put one or two Bible passages into 'modern dress' i.e. apply the Scriptures to modern life with its joys, pains and dilemmas.

3   Use Bible passages as an inspiration for poetry, calligraphy, collage, printing, banner-making . . .

4   Obtain a pile of newspapers. Scan through and tear out those stories which illustrate some great Bible themes, e.g.

   * forgiveness
   * love
   * reconciliation
   * human sinfulness
   * human dignity – we are made in the image of God

   (a) In what ways do these stories move, inspire or challenge you?

   (b) In what way do these stories illustrate the truths of the Bible?

5   Devise other practical group activities based on the Bible (and let John Young know what these are so that he can spread the word!).

For All

Ask a group member to read the following paragraph out loud.

Normally we read as quickly as possible, because we are reading newspapers, light fiction, etc. Or when we are studying a subject, we read as critically as possible. For a change, try reading suitable parts of the Bible as lovingly as possible – lingering over the scene, noticing every detail as if you had been there, asking what it shows you of God. Such 'meditation' on the Bible supplies a solid basis for prayer – and life. When you have got clearer in your mind the reality of God, coming to you in Jesus, stepping out of the pages of the Bible, you will find it easier to put together the jigsaw puzzle of your life. (David L. Edwards, former Provost of Southwark Cathedral)

Invite group members to sit in silence with eyes closed for three to five minutes while you do what David Edwards suggests, after reading Luke 24:13–35.

To close, say together the Collect for Bible Sunday.

Blessed Lord,
who caused all holy Scriptures to be written for our learning:
help us so to hear them,
to read, mark, learn, and inwardly digest them
that, through patience, and the comfort of your holy word,
we may embrace and for ever hold fast the hope of everlasting life,
which you have given us in our Saviour Jesus Christ. Amen.

SESSION 5: THE DYNAMIC

Ask people what lies at the centre of the Christian faith and many will point to the example and moral teaching of Jesus, especially the Sermon on the Mount (Matt. 5–7).

Clearly, they are not wrong – but they are not right either! The example of Jesus and his moral teaching are very important indeed. But they need to be put alongside another great truth . . .

In his letter to the Colossians, the apostle Paul speaks of 'God's secret'. It is an open secret. Some translations use the word 'mystery' – a secret hidden for centuries but now revealed for all to see. God's secret is this, says the apostle: 'Christ in you, the hope of glory' (Col. 1:27).

This is a wonderful truth. The Christian faith is not only a matter of following a matchless example, or trying to put high moral teaching into practice. If it was, we should be pretty miserable. For we all need far more than a fine example and lofty teaching, which show us just how feeble we are. We need inspiration, guidance, encouragement, forgiveness and inner strength. All these things – and more – are on offer. No wonder the writers of the New Testament describe their message, not as *good advice* but as *good news*.

Being a Christian means . . . being people in whom his [Jesus'] life and character and power are manifest and energised . . . Christian experience is not so much a matter of imitating a leader . . . as accepting and receiving a new quality of life – a life infinitely more profound and dynamic and meaningful than human life without Christ. (Harry Williams, Anglican monk)

To put this same truth in a slightly different way . . . Christianity is an Easter faith. We can sum up the Christian good news in three statements.

God is love.   Jesus is alive.   Death is dead.

God raised Jesus from the dead. So he is alive and active in our world – not just by his teaching but by his living presence. Jesus lives in us, in his Church and in his world, by his Spirit. He is unseen but very real.

The Bible uses many titles for the Spirit of Jesus. The best known is 'the Holy Spirit'. When we speak about the Holy Spirit, we are referring to the Spirit of Jesus himself (Acts 16:7). He comes into our lives

- to encourage us
- to reassure us
- to strengthen us
- to pray through us
- to enable us
- to challenge us
- to guide us
- to change us

The New Testament speaks of the *fruit of the Spirit* in our lives and the *gifts of the Spirit* within the Church.

- **The fruit of the Spirit** In a famous Bible verse, St Paul lists nine kinds of fruit which God wants to grow within our lives. (Look up Galatians 5:22–3.) He wants to grow every one of these lovely qualities within the life of every single believer. This reminds us that Christianity is a very practical business. The Holy Spirit is concerned about our daily lives, our personal relationships, and our priorities.
- **The gifts of the Spirit** The gifts of the Spirit are spread out among all members of the Church (the Greek word literally means 'dolloped out'!). No one has all the gifts; everyone has at

least one. They are given to us 'for the common good'. In this way God reminds us that *we need one another*. The Church is functioning properly when we work as a team. This is what Paul means when he speaks of the Church as 'the body of Christ' (1 Cor. 12:27).

- *The work of the Spirit*   We learn from the New Testament that the Holy Spirit is active in our world and in our lives. In *Know Your Faith* (Hodder & Stoughton) I listed eleven of his activities. Here I want to touch on two. First the Spirit points us to Jesus. He is 'a witness'.

> The work of the Holy Spirit is to draw attention to Jesus . . . therefore when we think about the Holy Spirit, we should not think about a kind of vague aura which produces a sort of emotion. The Spirit is much more precise than that. He brings to mind the truth, and he works out of us and with us and in us the moral implications of the truth. (Dr Donald English)

Second, the Spirit sets us to work. It is true that the Holy Spirit working within us can make us feel good. The seventeenth-century mathematician Blaise Pascal described his experience in these terms: 'Fire . . . certitude . . . peace . . . joy . . . tears of joy'. (It is also true that the Spirit can make us feel bad. He can convict us of sin and make us very uncomfortable.)

But the Spirit's main concern is not to make us *feel* good but to *do* good – to follow Jesus' 'new commandment' to love one another. The *teaching* of Jesus points us in a certain direction; the *Spirit* of Jesus provides energy – empowers us – to move in that direction (see, for example, Acts 1:8).

Ideas for Groups
For Discussion
1   Look around your group. Spend a few moments (in silence) reflecting on these questions.

- Which gift(s) do you think God has given to the various members 'for the common good'? Swop your ideas.
- Which gift(s) do you think God has given *you personally* 'for the common good'?

Ask (if you dare!) if other group members agree with you.

2 The New Testament speaks about believers as 'the temple of the Holy Spirit'.

- Look up 1 Corinthians 3:16 and 6:19.
- What do you think these phrases mean in practice?

3 Read Romans 8:15–17. George Thomas expressed the faith which comes from 'the spirit of sonship' when he said, 'My Christian faith is the spur to my every endeavour and my source of strength in trouble.' Share your own experiences, doubts and faith in the light of this.

4 In a couple of weeks you will have ended this short course. Do you plan to keep going as a group, or break up and get involved in other more permanent church groups, or . . . ?

5 'The Holy Spirit may without exaggeration be called the heartbeat of the Christian, the life-blood of the Christian Church' (The Doctrine Commission of the Church of England). Do you feel the force of this – or is this kind of language a closed book for you?

For Action

1 Copy out a prayer or hymn to the Holy Spirit, on card, for framing and hanging. Or write your own prayer to the Spirit of Jesus.

2 Read the following passage and design a collage, picture or banner based on the Holy Spirit.

Every biblical picture of the Holy Spirit is a moving one: the *seal* marks us as in the process of receiving the full inheritance; the *rain* must fall; the *river* flow; the *dew* descend; the *Spring of water* well up; the *fountain* rise; the *fire* must burn; the *oil* must flow; the *Dove* must fly.

For hundreds of years, through their bars, prisoners have gazed at birds in flight and longed for liberty. There has never been a more potent symbol of freedom. Ever since Noah, the Dove has been the sign of peace. So the Dove in flight is living promise of both freedom and peace, to Jesus, and through him, to us . . .

The Holy Spirit is always drawn to those who humble themselves before God. As water seeks the lowest level, so the Spirit flows to the most humble heart. (Eric Delve)

For All

Read Romans 8:26–7. Invite members to pray out loud, using one-sentence prayers. Close by saying or singing together

> Spirit of the Living God,
> Fall afresh on me.
> Spirit of the Living God,
> Fall afresh on me.
> Break me, melt me,
> Mould me, fill me.
> Spirit of the Living God,
> Fall afresh on me.

SESSION 6: THE OUTCOME

Service . . .

One of the most powerful verses in the New Testament is tucked away in Ephesians 4: 'He who has been stealing must steal no longer, but must work, doing something useful with his own hands, that he may have something to share with those in need' (v. 28).

At first sight it looks as though this has little to say to most of us, for only a handful of people reading *Explore Your Faith* are likely to be converted thieves! But scholars tell us that Ephesians was probably written as a circular letter and passed from church to church. In other words, it looks as though converted crooks could be found in most congregations.

Once again we are reminded of the power of the Gospel to radically transform twisted and broken lives. This power continues today. I know several one-time thieves who are now honest citizens as a result of coming to faith in Christ.

One of these is Fred Lemon (who, perhaps inevitably, became a greengrocer!). He was dramatically converted while planning a murder in his prison cell. On his release from prison, he and his wife adopted five needy children. It was their way of responding to Ephesians 4:28. In this very practical way they said 'thank you' to God for his love, mercy and forgiveness – and for giving them a wonderful new start in life.

Practical service of this kind is not only for converted crooks. *Every disciple* of Jesus is called to serve our troubled and divided world, in his name and through his strength. It will certainly mean giving money to help refugees and those facing starvation and grinding poverty. (Many Christian organisations will channel such gifts.) And it means working hard at being good neighbours and loyal friends.

Discipleship will also involve us in caring for our environment. 'Be kind to your local planet', as a poster on a teenager's wall put it. And it means dutiful citizenship, paying taxes and all that kind of boring stuff which is so important for a stable society. But it does not mean being bland! In the New Testament, Christians are described as 'soldiers'. We are called to fight against evil – in the world and within ourselves.

Think of William Wilberforce and Martin Luther King. Both were outstanding Christian leaders; both were thorns in the side of the establishment. There is nothing inconsistent about seeking to *change* the law while living *within* the law. And there is a long Christian tradition which says that conscience may lead you to break bad laws, providing you are willing to suffer the consequences. If this worries you, ask yourself: 'Would I have obeyed every order of Adolf Hitler, if I had lived in Germany in the 1940s?'

. . . and Witness

But practical service is only part of our calling. We are also called to witness to our faith in Jesus Christ.

An Asian Christian, D.T. Niles, defined evangelism as 'one beggar showing another beggar where he found bread'. A statement attributed to Mother Teresa runs like this: 'evangelism means to carry Jesus in your heart and to give the presence of Jesus to someone else'.

When we hear good news, we want to share it with others. 'Have you heard – Fred and Mary are engaged!' 'Isn't it wonderful that Jim and Jane have had a baby girl.' In the same way, the good news of God's love revealed to us in Jesus is too good to keep to ourselves. It must be passed on. But it is too precious to be handled roughly. The passing on of this news needs to be done boldly – and with sensitivity and humility. We can do this in two ways:

- *By our lives* New Christians often find that faith in Jesus makes a profound difference to their attitudes and actions. This is what close family and friends said about some recent new adult Christians:
  - 'You tackle things in a different way and your value system has changed.'
  - 'You're not so snappy, you look happier.'
  - 'Bigotry!'
  - 'I'm pleased for you – you look so happy.'

- 'You haven't half changed since you started going to church.'
- 'You're far less critical and quick-tempered.'
- 'It proves that you're weird.'
- 'A friend says she envies the amount of peace I have over things in life.'
- As St Francis put it: 'Preach the gospel; use words if you must.'
- **By our lips**   Sooner or later we shall find an opportunity to talk about our deepest beliefs.

None of this means that every Christian is called to be an evangelist. David Watson made this point with typical clarity. 'It is important to stress that not every Christian is called to be an evangelist. All are witnesses to Christ; all must be committed to the Church's task of evangelism; but only some are evangelists.'

This is not intended to be a 'let-out' for the half-hearted! Every single Christian belongs to an inescapably missionary Church. Every believer without exception is called to be a disciple of Jesus and a joyful witness to the love of God. But only a minority have that specific calling by God to be an evangelist.

I can think of three essential differences between an evangelist and a witness. (Do you agree? Can you think of others?) First, an evangelist is able to *create* opportunities for speaking about the Gospel; a witness is more comfortable *responding* to an initiative from someone else (1 Pet. 3:15). Second, a witness works best at evangelism in a team; an evangelist will often take individual initiatives. Third, an evangelist is able to handle 'God's story' (the Bible and history). A witness is equipped to handle his/her own story – to bear witness to the difference which God's love has made in his/her own life. 'Human story touches human story in the midst of God's story', as the Anglican Archbishops put it.

If I am right, the way forward is rooted in the notion of the Church as the body of Christ. The key is *team-work*. The image of the lonely 'personal evangelist', speaking freely about Jesus to friends, family and neighbours, is likely to raise guilt levels, for most of us are not good at this. So we see the importance of an outward-looking Church which enables the woman and man in the pew to bear witness to their faith in Jesus Christ.

The single most successful evangelistic strategy ever devised is very simple. It involves every individual Christian saying from time to time to an interested friend, neighbour or relative: 'I'm going; it's going to be good. Will you come with me?' We don't need super-special events to make this possible. Harvest festivals and carol services are just as useful as large central meetings.

Joan's Story

I used to work in an office. Like many people in Britain today, I had no real links with the Church and I didn't think very much about God – although I believed that he was there somewhere in the background. One day a new girl came to work in our office. Somehow she seemed 'different'. She was pleasant and sociable but she wouldn't take part in the office gossip.

As I got to know her better she told me about her church and her personal faith in Jesus Christ. One day she invited me along. I now share Ann's faith in Jesus and I am tremendously grateful to her for witnessing to me. I guess she's a little bit grateful to me too, for I introduced Ann to my brother, who is now her husband!

Since then, God has called me to serve him in interesting places like Afghanistan – and York!

Anne acted as a 'bridge' for Joan. See the lovely statement in Question 6 on p. 127.

Ideas for Groups
For Discussion

1   Can you help each other to find new opportunities for *personal* service

   • to the wider world?

- to friends and neighbours?

Repeat this question with your *group* in mind.

2   Some *church members* find that they can do together what they cannot do alone, e.g. some churches run soup kitchens or support loan clubs. Others run parent and toddler groups or provide lunches for old people. What are the needs and opportunities in your area?

3   Some churches find that they can offer as *churches working together* what they cannot do apart. One particular opportunity might be youth work. Recent research has shown that the church is losing touch with more and more of the nation's children and young people. Could groups of churches club together and pay the salary of a full- or part-time youth or schools' worker?
Could *your* group initiate this in your area?

4   A question from Donald English: 'Which people most helped you to become a Christian and how was that help given?' What can you learn from this concerning your own Christian witness to others?

5   Ponder this statement by Pope John Paul II. Reflect on your own experience in the light of his words. 'Missionary activity renews the Church, revitalises faith and Christian identity, and offers fresh enthusiasm and new incentives. Faith is strengthened when it is given to others.'

6   'My friend is rather shy, but she formed a bridge and Jesus Christ walked over it.' Discuss this statement made by a new Christian. (See also James Lawrence's statement on p. 142.)

For Action

Can you, as a group, arrange an evangelistic event to which you might invite friends, e.g. a supper party at which there will be a short talk (a testimony, perhaps)? Or make personalised invitation cards to invite friends to your harvest festival or carol service or . . . ?

How can this strange story of God made man, of a crucified saviour, of resurrection and new creation, become credible for those whose entire mental training has conditioned them to believe that the real world is the world which can be satisfactorily explained and managed without the hypothesis of God? I know of only one clue to the answering of that question . . . a congregation which believes it . . . (Bishop Lesslie Newbigin)

For All

Sit quietly, then say together the following prayer:

Lord Jesus Christ, you looked upon the city of Jerusalem with sadness and tears. Look with mercy upon our town/ city/village and surrounding countryside and help us with one voice to gladden many hearts with the good news of your love and grace. Amen.

SECOND SUMMARY:

What it Means to Be a Christian

The early followers of Jesus were first called Christians by other people – probably as a nickname (Acts 11:26). They gladly accepted this title, because it declared to the whole world that they were Christ's people.

What does it mean to be a Christian? It means accepting Jesus as Teacher and Saviour, and worshipping him as Lord and God. It means following the instruction of the letter to the Hebrews: 'Let us keep our eyes fixed on Jesus, upon whom our faith depends from beginning to end' (Heb. 12:2). *With that verse in mind we can see that being a Christian means:*

- *Studying the teaching and example of Jesus*   In the Gospels Jesus is often called 'Teacher'. From his teaching and example we learn the secret of living a fully human life.

  – He wants us to relate to other people in forgiveness and love by putting harsh judgements on the back burner.

  – He shows us how to relate to God as Father. We are to trust God, to love God and to fear God, i.e. to stand in awe of his greatness and love.

  – He calls us to serve our troubled and divided world. Jesus turns our standards upside down. The most important people are the poor and vulnerable. We are to be generous with our time, energy, talents and money. These are gifts from God: we are to use them in his service.

  All this we learn from a loving, leisurely study of the Gospels, the most influential documents in the history of the world.

- *Praying to the Father of Jesus*   'Lord, teach us to pray' requested his first disciples. In reply, Jesus uttered the world's most famous prayer. It begins, 'Our Father in heaven . . .' God is *holy* – so we come humbly, confessing our sins. God is *love* – so we come joyfully, rejoicing in his forgiveness. God is *our Father* – so we come boldly, to share with him our worries and joys, and to pray for the needs of other people.

- **Kneeling at the cross of Jesus**   How much do you love your world, Lord? To answer this question, Jesus opened his arms to embrace us all. Lawless man took those arms and nailed them to a cross. In our imagination we kneel humbly at the place where the cost of our redemption is so clearly displayed.

  – Here we see *the love of God*. Jesus died for *you* – and for me. 'God so loved the world that he gave his one and only Son' (John 3:16).

  – Here we see *the depth of human sin*. The cross declares, 'You have deep and desperate needs, requiring *this* remedy.'

  – Here we see *the cost of Christian discipleship*. 'Follow me,' said Jesus. Then he got himself crucified. Being a Christian always involves a sort of death. For it means enthroning Jesus – not ourselves – as King of our lives.

  – Here we see *the way back to God*. Only the death of Jesus could break down the barriers of rebellion and indifference, which separate people from God and from one another.

- **Rejoicing in the resurrection of Jesus**   Being a Christian means sharing a joyful, confident view of life. We do not worship a dead hero; we rejoice in a living Lord. Being a Christian means looking back thankfully to the life, death and resurrection of Jesus. It means walking with the risen Lord, day by day. And it means looking forward hopefully to the vibrant life of heaven.

- **Drawing strength from the Spirit of Jesus**   Jesus makes tough demands. But we are not on our own. He is with us – by his Spirit, the Holy Spirit (Matt. 28:20). Jesus gives us strength for living. We develop a growing awareness of his presence – guiding, challenging, inspiring and renewing us.

- **Belonging to the family of Jesus**   We need one another. Church is not an optional extra. Being a Christian means giving encouragement to other believers, and receiving support from them. We gather *as a family* – for worship and for fellowship. Archbishop George Carey put it like this: 'It is impossible to be a Robinson Crusoe Christian. We need the human family in order to live and grow and similarly we need the Christian family to grow as Christians.'

- **Submitting to the Lordship of Jesus**   Provost David Edwards sums this up very clearly: 'By dying like that, Jesus has won the right to be "our Lord". The word "lord" here means "boss". There are many ways of defining what "a Christian" is. The best one is this: a Christian is one who takes orders from Jesus Christ as Lord.'

- **Witnessing to the love of Jesus**   God is love; death is dead; Jesus is alive! These great truths are too wonderful to keep to ourselves. Good news is for sharing. Being a Christian means doing this humbly, sensitively and confidently – in fellowship with other believers.

(Note: The first Summary may be found on p. 24.)

A real Christian is not only a good and well-intentioned person but a man or woman for whom Jesus Christ is ultimately decisive; for whom Jesus – not Caesar, not another god, not money, sex, power, or pleasure – is Lord. (Professor Hans Küng)

What a tremendous relief . . . to discover that we don't need to prove ourselves to God. That is what Jesus came to say, and for that he got killed . . . The Good News is that God loves me long before I could have done anything to deserve it. He is like the father of the prodigal son, waiting anxiously for the return of his wayward son . . . That is tremendous stuff – that is the Good News. Whilst we were yet sinners, says St Paul, Christ died for us. God did not wait until we were die-able, for He could have waited until the cows came home. (Archbishop Desmond Tutu)

FIFTH COURSE

Evangelism without an Evangelist

INTRODUCTION

Before becoming Bishop of Pontefract in 1993, John Finney was National Officer for Evangelism in the Church of England. In 1992 he published research on how 511 adults in modern Britain came to faith in Jesus Christ. His research was published in a book entitled Finding Faith Today *(Bible Society, 1992). It has been − and continues to be − extremely influential. In an attempt to turn the findings into practical action at local level, John asked me to write a workbook which was also published by the Bible Society as* Journeys Into Faith. *What follows is a course from that book based on John Finney's work, and I am extremely grateful to the Bible Society for granting permission for this material to appear in this amended form.*

> There is an audio-tape which accompanies this course, available from York Courses (for address see p. x). Unlike the previous four courses, however, the cassette is not an integral part of the course but acts as a supplement to it. The tapes consist of interviews with leading figures in the world of evangelism, including the Revd Brian Hoare, the Revd Robin Gamble, Bishop Gavin Reid and Canon Robert Warren.

Note to leaders: You may wish to spread each session over two meetings.

SESSION 1: HOW THEY CAME IN

Introduction
A total of 511 adults who had recently come to faith in Jesus Christ took part in John Finney's research, and they were asked some searching questions. They were from all the mainstream churches, from Roman Catholic to House Church (sometimes called New Church), and had recently been baptised, confirmed or received into church membership as adults. Among other things, they were asked:

- What was the main factor used by God to bring you to faith?
- What were the supporting factors?

Task 1: Think and Write
Give out three different coloured slips of paper to members of your group. Ask members to think about their own pilgrimage to faith (or *towards* faith if they are enquirers rather than believers). Then ask them . . .
- On one piece to write *the main one or two factors* which brought them to faith in Christ (e.g. a special mission, a person, an organisation, an experience).
- On the second piece of paper to list any *supporting factors*.
- On the third slip to list factors which they know to be important *for other people*, i.e. what are some of the rungs on the 'ladder of experience' which lead people to an active faith in God?

Invite members of the group to share their findings or (if you have a shy group) collect them in.

The results for the 511 who took part in the national survey are shown below. Respondents were allowed more than one supporting factor.

	Main factor	Supporting factor
Friends	21%	40%
Family members	27%	47%
Family made up of:		
Partner/spouse	11%	16%
Own children	9%	14%
Parents	6%	13%
Other family members	1%	11%
Minister	17%	43%
The Bible	5%	27%
Church activities	6%	34%
Evangelistic event	4%	13%
Christian lay person	4%	13%
A dream or vision	3%	3%
TV or radio	–	6%
Literature, drama, music	2%	16%
Other	11%	6%

Task 2: Compare
- Are there many differences in the factors listed by your group and those in the survey?
- Do the factors and figures surprise you, or are they what you would expect?

Times and Seasons
Are there certain times in life when we are more open to the Gospel? Yes! Most of us plod along without giving too much thought to deeper issues until something wonderful, shattering or challenging happens. Events which got people in the research group thinking hard were: moving house, getting engaged or married, giving birth, bereavement.

Task 3: Questions
- Does this link with your experience or the experience of other people known to you?
- Can you extend the list of key events?

Of Earthly Use?

What is the Church here for? Many modern firms have a 'mission statement' (a term borrowed from the Church) or 'vision statement'. This is a crisp summary of what the company is trying to do. A group of clergy were invited to draw up their own mission statements. One minister had a go and ran a 'can you do better?' competition in his church magazine. He wrote that the parish purpose is:

> Through the living of the Christian Faith to call, enable and encourage all who are within its bounds, to turn to Christ, repent of wrong and renounce evil, and so to come to fulfil Jesus' command that human beings should love God with all their heart, all their strength, all their mind and all their soul, and their neighbours as themselves.

Task 4: Take Aim
- One parishioner gave the vicar's offering (above) a tongue-in-cheek 2 out of 10! What would you award it?
- Each group member draw up a mission statement for your church. Swop your attempts, refine and offer the finished product to your church leaders.

Task 5

What are the implications of all this for you as an individual/
for your group/for your church/for your local group of
churches, as you seek to reach out with the good news of
Jesus Christ?

- Many people in the survey spoke of the importance of
  Christian ministers, speaking warmly of their approach-
  ability and integrity. Might you organise a 'Meet Our
  Minister' evening (or morning/afternoon) at which questions can be put, he/she could speak about his/her faith
  and work, and life story?

- What about newcomers to your area? Could you devise a
  'holy spy' network? i.e. members keep a sharp eye for
  removal vans and greet newcomers with a cake, a pack of
  information about your district and church, and an offer
  of help.

Sharing Comes Naturally

He enjoyed the joke and couldn't wait to pass it on. She had a
really good holiday and was anxious to recommend it to her friends.
I needed to replace my car and was grateful for his recommenda-
tion. She had a baby girl and her sister spent the evening on the
phone, telling friends.

These examples of good news being passed on tell us something
important about what it means to be human. Most of us want to
share our enthusiasms. Passing on those things which are important
to us is a vital aspect of personal relationships. Evangelism is simply
a part of all this. How can we draw the line at something as glorious
as the 'glad tidings of great joy' (Luke 2:10)?

But the means must be appropriate to the end. God does not
force; he invites. So it should be with us. Let us be bold and
imaginative in our evangelism; but let us not be pushy and ill-
mannered. Open-air evangelism or distributing leaflets can be
appropriate and effective. Even 'custard-pie evangelism' – shouting
loudly in the hope that something 'sticks' – can be effective. But

the good news sounds like bad news to those on the receiving end, if they feel cornered.

Evangelism is not intellectual imperialism. The Christian faith is not a package to be delivered with a hard sell. It is rooted in love and friendship. It is about sensitive invitation and considered response. It is about confidence in the Holy Spirit to bring people to faith in Jesus Christ and to transform their lives – and ours too.

Ponder and Pray
- Read John 1:35–42 in which Andrew introduces Simon Peter to Jesus.
- Each pray for two or three friends.

SESSION 2: WHAT THEY FOUND

'Belonging precedes believing' (Professor Robin Gill).

The 511 meant business. They realised that the Christian faith means a lot more than a coat of religious varnish. Most of them wanted to get stuck into church life. *Take heart*: 80 per cent of those who already had occasional contact with the Church found it easy to get involved in church life. Two-thirds of those with no previous church links found it easy. *But don't get complacent*: this means that one-third of those with no previous church links found it hard to get involved. This figure was taken from those who persevered – it is quite possible that other enquirers fled after the first contact. Consider the churches that you know – especially your own. Can you think of one that is outstanding in its efforts to make newcomers welcome?

Task 1: Hot or Cold?

How would you rate your church on a friendship scale *among church members*:
VERY FRIENDLY; QUITE FRIENDLY; COOL; UN-FRIENDLY?

How would you rate your church on a friendship scale *with reference to outsiders*:
VERY FRIENDLY; QUITE FRIENDLY; COOL; UN-FRIENDLY?

Give examples from your own experience, or from the experience of other people, to support your views.

- One woman tried very hard to join a local church. She was frozen out – not by cold, unfriendly people, but by people who were preoccupied with their own internal friendships. Could this happen in your church?
- On the other hand, consider the experience of a man in his early twenties who spent three years in prison for robbery with violence. He came to faith in prison and on being released he looked for a church. He realised that it was asking a lot for 'normal' church members to accept someone with his background. But they did – and he was very grateful. How would your church respond to such a request?
- Draw up a list of practical steps which you might take (as an *individual*, as a *group* and as a *church*) to make newcomers more welcome.

You might act out a role play with someone taking the part of an enquirer attending church for the first time. You are allowed to exaggerate!

Marks of a Growing Church

David Winter studied fourteen growing churches in the Oxford diocese. They shared ten features. To summarise: as well as announcing good news, the church must *be* good news in its locality, if it is to be taken seriously. Parent and toddler groups, visits to the elderly, help for the homeless, lunches for the needy – all are signs of a caring church. What might be appropriate in *your* situation?

Read David Winter's list* and consider your own church life in the light of these factors. Ask each member to write the appropriate letters against each feature: VG (very good), G (good), A (average), P (Poor). Then compare answers. If you feel strongly about any of

*Taken from *By Word and Deed* edited by Colin Craston, Church House Publishing (1992).

these issues, why not attend your next church AGM or write a careful letter to your leaders?

1   Care for the needy within the congregation.
2   Structures (e.g. small groups for the open sharing of faith by members of the congregation).
3   The ability to manage change within the church.
4   A collaborative style of leadership.
5   Emphasis on prayer.
6   Good giving of money.
7   Lively, varied and sincere worship.
8   A concern for, and action within, the locality.
9   The setting of clear and realisable objectives and regular reviews of church strategy.
10 The sense that the laity is to be the Church in the world and not just clerical helpers within the congregation (i.e. an outward-looking rather than an inward-looking attitude).

The English Church Census (Marc Europe, 1991) revealed much the same. Eight common features of growing churches were:

- easy accessibility
- real friendship
- relevant worship
- involvement in community
- independent leaders
- emphasis on evangelism
- attractive image
- integration of family

Note: A great deal of work has been done in this area recently. For Canon Robert Warren's *Characteristics of Healthy Churches* contact York Courses (see p. x). The *Natural Church Development Handbook* by Christian A. Schwarz (BCGA, 1998) is also relevant.

Task 2
- How do churches in your area relate to the findings in these two surveys?
- On the audio-tape for Course 3, Steve Chalke mentions research which suggests that a common feature of growing churches is that they *laugh* a lot! What do you think about this?

Task 3: Taking the Temperature
- Could you, as a group, invite a few friends who are not members of your church to attend for one, two or three Sundays without acknowledging their friendship with you?
- Draw up a list of questions and a score card and ask them to fill it in.
  - Were you welcomed by church members?
  - Were you welcomed by church officials?
  - Were you suffocated by attention or was it just right?
  - Could you find your way around the service?
  - Did what you found make you want to come back?
- Who might you ask to do this? Which other questions would you use?
- How might you use this information in a constructive way within your church (no negative grumbling please!)?
- Is your church growing numerically, shrinking, or standing still? Why?
- Do you think it is right to be concerned with numerical growth?

Ponder and Pray

It is easy to speak or write about evangelism as though it were merely a human activity – persuading others to join us as Christians. The New Testament is clear, however, that there is more to it than meets the eye. It is about a spiritual warfare for which spiritual weapons are needed. Amongst these, prayer figures highly. (Donald English)

Evangelisation involves a personal and profound meeting with the Saviour . . . [it] involves conversion, that is, interior change.

Missionary activity renews the Church, revitalises faith and Christian identity, and offers fresh enthusiasm and new incentives. Faith is strengthened when it is given to others. (Pope John Paul II)

There is no true evangelisation if the name, the teaching, the life, the promises, the kingdom and the mystery of Jesus of Nazareth, the Son of God, are not proclaimed. (Pope Paul VI)

Evangelism involves faithfulness to the opportunity God gives us to accompany someone on the next step of the journey to faith. (James Lawrence)

Set us free, O God, to cross barriers for you, as you crossed barriers for us, in Jesus Christ our Lord. Amen. (URC prayer)

SESSION 3: OVER TO YOU

Some people come to faith in God in a dramatic way – by means of a 'voice' or compelling inner experience. Here are examples from the survey:

> I was reading the gospel according to Mark. When I read about the crucifixion I had an indescribable feeling which included a combination of fear, ecstasy and awe. I knew that Jesus Christ was with me.

> I had a series of very vivid dreams . . . Jesus took me down a set of very grand stairs, opened a very large door and guided me to a road which forked. One fork of the road was not signposted and the other fork was signposted and said, 'Jesus'.

Task 1: Share Experiences
- Have any members of your group had dramatic experiences of this kind?
- The research shows very clearly that most people come to faith by much more ordinary means – especially through the influence of family and friends. Ask members of your group to share experiences of this more 'ordinary' kind.

Evangelism without an Evangelist
Christians don't need to be 'evangelists' to help bring their friends to faith in Christ. But they do need to be five things:

- *Normal* People often express surprise that Christians – especially clergy – are normal people! The caricature, gained perhaps from television, has a strong and pervasive influence which can only be destroyed by meeting real people.

- *Different*   In addition to normality, people outside the Church are often impressed by faith which connects with real life. They see something 'different' and desirable in the Christian life.
- *Sensitive*   'They didn't continually force their opinions and ideas down my throat which would have irritated me. They showed me their love by befriending me and this was very important,' said a woman in the survey.
- *Bold*   'She asked me to go to church with her; I was pleasantly surprised,' said another participant.
- *Patient*   On average it took about four years of positive encounters with Christians and church before most 'outsiders' were ready to take a step of commitment.

Task 2: Look in a Mirror
Give yourself a score for each of the above five points on a scale of 1–10 (10 = very good; 1 = very poor). Then exchange scores with other members of the group. The purpose is to see if you can help each other to improve your score by one or two notches. (*Suggestion*: don't ask your partners whether they agree with your scores. We don't want to lose friends!)

Down with Guilt

It would be very sad if the mention of evangelism simply made church members feel guilty ('another day gone and I haven't spoken to ten people about the Lord'!). The following quotation from an outstanding British evangelist might help. 'It is important to stress that not every Christian is called to be an evangelist. All are witnesses to Christ; all must be committed to the Church's task of evangelism; but only some are evangelists' (David Watson).

David Watson did not intend this to be a let-out! *Every* Christian is an agent of mission who belongs to an inescapably missionary Church. *Every* believer is called to be a disciple of Jesus and a witness to the love of God. So what are the differences between an evangelist and a witness? Here are three possibilities:

- *An evangelist* is able to *create* opportunities to talk about the faith.
  A witness is able to *respond* to questions (look up 1 Peter 3:15).
- *An evangelist* can work *solo* as well as in a team.
  A witness is able to slot into church outreach as a *team member* –
  issuing invitations, putting out chairs, distributing leaflets, taking
  part in surveys, helping to prepare people for baptism and
  marriage, speaking about his or her life and faith, cooking for
  faith-sharing suppers, making coffee, knocking on doors . . .
- *An evangelist* is able to handle '*God's* story' (the Bible and history)
  with confidence.
  Witnesses are able to tell *their own story*, i.e. the importance of
  their personal faith for their lives.

The key is team work. We can do *together* what we can't do apart.
'You are the body of Christ' (1 Cor. 12:27). This is why it is so
important for a church to have a sense of direction and practical
schemes for evangelism – these enable us to work together in
making Christ known.

Task 3: Look Around
- Which members of your group have a gift for evangelism?
  Which (the rest!) are called to be witnesses?
- Do you think the distinction between the two is helpful –
  or an easy escape for the lazy?
- Would you add any other points to the three differences
  listed above?
- What are the particular problems and encouragements for
  Christian witness at work and at home?
- Do you, or have you, suffered persecution or ridicule for
  your faith – or do you find that most people respect most
  Christians?

Further Practical Ideas

1 *Brainstorm*

The most successful single strategy for evangelism is for one Christian to say to a friend, neighbour or relative: 'I'm going. It's going to be good. Will you come with me?'

- List a few church activities to which you might invite one or two friends (carol service, harvest supper, ecumenical celebration, etc.) Or
- Organise an 'Outreach Supper' (in a home or hired room at a pub) with visiting speaker.
- Each individual draws up a list of friends whom they might invite.
- Pray together for these individuals.
- Design and produce attractive invitation cards for use at the next major church festival event. Ask if you can give out three cards to each member of your congregation for use among their friends.
- Revisit any sections from Sessions 1 or 2 which you have not yet tackled.

2 *Taking the Gospel out*

Some churches find that they are welcome in a local pub or social club if they organise a service (e.g. harvest, carols) or informal singing. For other ideas see the Booklist on p. ii.

3 *Consider and Discuss*

Do you agree/disagree/can you illustrate/would you modify any of the following three key statements?

- We British Christians live in a tough mission field (contrast the Church in Nepal, which is doubling every three years).
- We belong to a timid Church.
- We live in a society which is interested in 'God questions' – morality, meaning, prayer, life-after-death, spirituality . . .

4 *Omission or Commission?*

Our witness to Christ need not (*should* not!) be 'heavy'. Consider these four lovely definitions of evangelism:

- 'Evangelism means to carry Jesus in your heart and to give the presence of Jesus to someone else' (attributed to Mother Teresa).
- 'Evangelism is one beggar showing another beggar where he found bread' (D.T. Niles, an Asian Christian).
- 'My friend is rather shy, but she formed a bridge and Jesus Christ walked over it' (one of the 511 interviewed in John Finney's research).
- 'Evangelism is helping people to belong so that they can believe' (Bishop John Finney).

That catches it perfectly. The Church is intended to be a bridge between Jesus and the world. Unfortunately, for too many Christians in the Western Church, the Great Commission has become the Great Omission. However, it *can* be done and there are many encouragements. Some churches are growing. People are coming to faith. As nominal members drop off the edge of church life, so more committed members come in. Hence John Finney was able to find a large number of new adult believers for his survey.

> When Chairman Mao imposed the Cultural Revolution, there were only about one million Christians in all of China. Today, Christians in China number from twenty to forty million.
>
> This great movement became possible because tens of thousands of lay people, a majority women, discovered their calling to succeed the apostles in outreach to people who are not yet believers. (George Hunter)
>
> It was the same for Rome and for Britain in the early days. The Gospel was heard in Rome and in Britain, not because a great evangelist preached, but because a small army of witnesses shared their faith. These were traders, sailors, soldiers, refugees, slaves . . .

It is always good to have an evangelist to hand, but they are an optional extra – a luxury! Only two things are essential for the Gospel to spread:

- Christian witnesses *and*
- a loving, believing community.

(See p. 128 for a relevant statement by Bishop Lesslie Newbigin.)

Close by reading Isaiah 52:7–12.

SESSION 4: THE 'C' WORD

What is slippery and usually pink, yellow or black in colour? I am not referring to a wet bar of soap but to a word – that word 'Christian'. Someone once challenged me: 'My friend is a Communist and an Atheist, but he's as good a Christian as you.' This has a positive side. He wanted to praise his friend so he used the word 'Christian'. This suggests something very positive about the followers of Jesus. However, it also has a negative side. Christians don't have a monopoly on goodness. So it is a bit confusing when people who don't follow Christ want to use a word which contains his name.

Task 1: Imagine
You meet a Buddhist who asks:
- Would you describe England as a Christian country?
- Is Christianity for good people or for bad people?
- What do you mean when you call someone a Christian?

Share your answers within the group.

Most of the 511 in the survey defined the word 'Christian' in terms of a relationship. They felt that they . . .

- had established a personal relationship with God;
- had a developing relationship (not always easy!) with other believers;
- were more at ease with themselves;
- viewed Jesus as friend and Saviour – someone to turn to and talk to.

Task 2: Basic Questions
1 Do you feel like that? Can you give examples or illustrations?
2 'There are many ways of defining what a Christian is. The best one is this: a Christian is one who takes orders from Jesus Christ as Lord' (David L. Edwards).
   • How would you rate this as a definition?
   • What might this mean for you? (be specific)
3 What would you say if someone asked you:
   • why should I become a Christian?
   • how can I become a Christian? (see pp. 24, 129)
4 You are in court. The charge against you is that you are a Christian.
   • What evidence would the prosecutor be able to bring *against* you?
   • What evidence would the defence be able to bring *for* you?

You might attempt to act this out.

Sudden or Gradual?
Some of the 511 were 'catapulted' into faith in a sudden experience on a particular day, like St Paul. But most weren't (see 2 Timothy 1:5). On average it took four years of interest and enquiry. Eventually they felt 'ready' to be baptised, confirmed or received into membership. Discuss in your group:

• How many 'suddens' and how many 'graduals' do you have in your group?
• How many 'suddens' would speak of a *process* leading up to the moment of decision or revelation?
• How many 'graduals' would speak of a *crystallising moment* when the penny dropped?
• What insights and strengths do the 'graduals' bring to the whole Church?

- What insights and strengths do the 'suddens' bring to the whole Church?

To End This Session
Ponder

That is why everyone is challenged to respond to God through Jesus Christ in a personal turning (which is what the word 'conversion' means). You have to meet Jesus yourself and to accept him as your friend and as your Lord. In many Christian lives, this turning or conversion reaches a climax which can be dated. People can remember the exact time when they accepted Jesus Christ as Lord and Liberator, but it is not necessary to be able to date your conversion like that.

What is essential is that everyone should have his or her personal reasons for being a Christian. You cannot inherit Christian faith as you can inherit red hair or a peculiar nose. You cannot copy Christian faith. Your faith, to be authentic, to guide your life, must be your own. Your very own experience, whether it is dramatic or quiet, long or short, must lead you to know Jesus Christ as your personal Liberator. (Provost David L. Edwards)

We all have to choose between two ways of being crazy; the foolishness of the Gospel and the nonsense of the values of this world. (Jean Vanier, founder of l'Arche)

Christianity is a statement which, if false, is of no importance, and if true, of infinite importance. The one thing it cannot be is moderately important. (C.S. Lewis)

. . . and Pray

Pray for your church, for your witness, for our troubled and divided world. Pray too that this glorious Gospel may fire our imaginations and warm our hearts.

SESSION 5: BEFORE AND AFTER

A Real Difference

The 511 new Christians in the survey meant business. Their new-found faith made a real difference to their lives. They attended church more often, read the Bible and prayed more regularly.

But radical changes did not occur only in these 'religious' areas. Most of the people in the survey felt very positive about what had happened to them. They felt more confident about life and about themselves. They had a clearer sense of direction.

- 'I'm not afraid of facing anything.'
- 'It's given life a point.'
- 'I'm more thoughtful, caring, tolerant, contented, aware of others' needs.'
- 'Never thought I'd be able to forgive people.'
- 'I am happier within myself.'
- 'I have given up working too hard at the wrong things.'
- 'Everything makes better sense now.'
- 'It's like having a sixth sense – seeing the world through new eyes.'
- 'I am more trustful of people. I don't worry so much about life.'
- 'My attitude towards people has changed drastically. I was a very catty person – always the first person to shout my mouth off. Now I'm always trying to make up . . . less moody.'

John Finney sums it up like this:

In nearly every case their newfound faith seems to have given them a greater sense of self-worth and they feel more at home in their own skin. Many speak of achieving a sense of purpose – 'before, it was a case of drifting'. They have found a peace of mind – 'I used to be on tranquillisers but I don't need them any more.' They felt they have some basis for life – 'I know there's more to life than drinking and messing about with girls.'

Task 1: How About You?
- Put a tick next to any of the statements on p. 152 with which you can identify and a cross against any which do not apply to you.
- How would you answer the question: What difference does the Christian faith make to *your* life?

Other People

Other people – especially parents and partners – seemed to endorse the positive judgements made by the respondents in the survey. There were critical comments, of course ('My wife says I am obsessed with Christianity') but most were appreciative. They ranged from the practical ('easier to live with') to this lovely testimonial from one husband: 'You've grown from a scared little girl to a beautiful confident woman.'

The less close people were to the new Christian, the more cynical their response was likely to be. The negative comments came mainly from those who were acquaintances.

- 'You go to church all the time now – it's all church, church, church.'
- 'Why don't you come down to the pub more often? (Though I do)'
- 'He's going through a mid-life crisis. You'll get over it soon.'
- 'I hope it's not contagious.'

There were plenty of other barbed comments and mockery.

Task 2: Making Links
- How does this link with your experience? Do you suffer for your faith? If so, look up Matthew 5:10–12. If not, is it because nobody outside church knows about your faith?
- How can we help believers – especially young people at school or college – who suffer for their faith?

Real Life

In 1992, Roy Castle discovered that he had lung cancer. He was given no more than a 10 per cent chance of pulling through. As a result of his Christian faith he was able to say that he was not afraid of death – although he viewed it as an enemy which would snatch him too early from family, friends and work. When asked to sum up the importance of his faith he wrote this: 'My Christian faith is most important to me because of its simplicity and perfect honesty. So many times I am tempted to be dissatisfied and jealous of others, but Christianity quickly dispels these evil suspicions and returns me to humility which brings that special peace.'

Roy Castle's faith engaged, not just with 'religion', but with the real stuff of real life – fear, facing death, jealousy.

Lord Tonypandy (George Thomas, a former Speaker of the House of Commons) put it like this: 'My Christian faith is the spur to my every endeavour and my source of strength in trouble.'

Task 3
- Discuss the areas of your life which you would pick out – those areas where your faith really makes contact.
- Which other areas of your life would you like your faith to engage with more than it does now?
- If, like Roy Castle, you were asked to sum up the importance of your faith in a couple of sentences – what would you write?

Bible Study

- Which people were vital for Timothy's Christian faith (see 2 Timothy 1:5)?
- Read about the sudden conversion of the apostle Paul (Acts 9). Then read about the death of Stephen (Acts 7:54–8:1). Do you think that Stephen's death and Saul's conversion are connected? Notice the result of persecution (Acts 8:1–4).

SESSION 6: WHAT IS THE GOSPEL?

Task 1: A Key Question

That Buddhist visitor again! He is interested in all things British and he visits your church. At the end he says, 'I hear much about the gospel and the good news. Please tell me – what is this Christian good news?'

• How would you answer this key question?

Sin and Guilt

The Bible talks a fair bit about sin and forgiveness and many evangelistic sermons focus on this. 'Repent and turn to Christ that your sins might be forgiven.' Of course, this is a vital message. *But* . . . according to this research, it doesn't 'connect' with the felt needs of many non-Christians.

In *Finding Faith Today*, John Finney writes:

> Only 39% said they had *any* sense of guilt . . . The picture of guilt-ridden, self-accusatory people finding psychological release by turning to Christianity is sometimes painted. If it is true at all, it is true for only a small minority – the great majority of the stories which the participants told did not major on this.

None of this means that the Bible message of sins forgiven is out-of-date. It does mean that this is not the *starting* point for many modern people. Indeed, it is often true that a sense of sin and the need for forgiveness grow *only after people are on the road to finding faith*. There are some famous examples of this. In *Surprised By Joy*, C.S. Lewis wrote about his experience as a young tutor at Oxford, when he was grappling with Christianity: 'For the first time I examined myself with a seriously practical purpose. And there I found what appalled me; a zoo of lusts, a bedlam of ambitions, a nursery of fears, a harem of fondled hatreds. My name was legion.'

Task 2
- Do you feel that this is over the top or can you recognise what C.S. Lewis is talking about?
- Do you have a growing sense of sin and unworthiness?
- Does this make you despair – or rejoice more and more in the good news of God's mercy and grace?
- Do you want to raise any other points arising from 'Sin and Guilt'?

Task 3
If a need for forgiveness is not the trigger for the journey to faith in God for many modern people, what is?

Is it . . . the search for meaning in life; a desire to make sense of experience; the need for moral and spiritual strength; an inability to cope with problems; grief; a sense of thankfulness for life and joy; loneliness; lack of peace; the inspiration of a believing friend . . . or what?

Grow Big, Grow Wild!

In the Bible, 'sin' means more than 'sins'. Sin is a whole attitude to life which shuts God out and puts other people's interests at the margins of our lives. A notice-board outside a cathedral declared, 'Sin is a refusal to grow bigger'. That sums it up. We sin when we settle for cautious mediocrity: when we keep our horizons low and settle for safety, rather than allowing God to lead us into adventurous faith.

It is wonderful when God tames wild people, like criminals and drug addicts. It is even more wonderful when faith in God causes tame people to become a bit more wild! How do you think *you* rate on a wild/tame scale? Put two arrows: one on the left-hand side for *where you are now*, one on the right-hand side to indicate *where God wants you to be*.

Task 4
Now   *Description*   *Then*
                       Very cautious
                       Quite cautious
                       Cautious
                       Fairly daring
                       Adventurous faith
                       Wild
                       Too wild!

Can you name two practical courses of action which might be involved (for you, or members of your group) under the heading 'Adventurous faith'?

Faith and Doubt

Faith and doubt are not only a question of *thinking* but of *feeling* and of *acting*.

The New Testament often speaks about *peace*. Faith has a passive side: 'Let go and let God.' If our faith is working, we are able to worry less and leave things with God rather more. The apostle Peter puts this very strongly: 'Cast all your anxiety on him [God], because he cares for you' (1 Pet. 5:7).

The New Testament speaks even more often about *faith in action*. Look up Hebrews 11 – a whole chapter on this. 'By faith Abraham . . . obeyed and went' (verse 8).

But, of course, faith does have its thinking aspects. The 511 did not have mega-struggles of this kind with their new-found faith. It was all so real that they were able to live with the questions which they could not answer, in the light of the answers which they had found.

Two problems which *did* surface were:

- the problem of suffering – why does God allow it?
- violence in the Old Testament

(John Young has discussed these issues elsewhere – see Booklist on p. ii.)

Task 5: Your Questions
- Are these problems for you?
- List additional questions which *you* would like to tackle.
- With 1 Peter 5:7 in mind, does your faith enable you to worry less?
- Does your faith result in obedient action, as it did for Abraham?

Task 6
Now turn to p. 129 and read the second Summary, using several voices.

Finally . . .
To Ponder and (Perhaps) Discuss
'Come, follow me,' Jesus said, 'and I will make you fishers of men' (Mark 1:17).

Now it came to pass that a group existed who called themselves fishermen. And lo, there were many fish in the waters all around. Week after week, these who called themselves fishermen met in meetings. They talked about their call to fish, the abundance of fish, and how they might go about fishing.

One thing they did not do; they did not fish.

After tedious training many graduated and were given fishing licences. They were sent to do full-time fishing, some to distant waters which were filled with fish. But like the fishermen back home, they never fished.

After one stirring meeting on 'The Necessity of Fishing'

one young fellow left the meeting and went fishing. The next day he reported that he had caught two outstanding fish. He was honoured for his excellent catch and scheduled to visit all the big meetings possible to tell how he did it. So he stopped his fishing in order to have time to talk about the experience to the other fishermen.

Now it is true that many of the fishermen sacrificed much and put up with all kinds of difficulties. Some lived near the water and bore the smell of dead fish every day. They received the ridicule of some who made fun of their fishermen's club.

Imagine how hurt some were when one day a person suggested that those who did not catch fish were not really fishermen, no matter how much they claimed to be. Yet it did sound correct. Is a person a fisherman if he never catches a fish? Is one following if he is not fishing?

Bill Thrasher (abridged)

- Pray as boldly as you dare! And take heart from the fact that a good deal of fishing *is* taking place, for the church of Jesus Christ world-wide is growing every day.
- All good wishes as you seek to help others to find faith today.

SIXTH COURSE

Foundations for Christian Living

SESSION 1: DISCIPLES LEARNING TO FOLLOW JESUS

A Course on Christian Discipleship *by the Revd Ian Parkinson, Vicar of Saltburn in North Yorkshire (see Preface and p. 184 for further details)*

The best description of what it means to be a Christian is the term which Jesus himself used of his own first followers. This word applies to every follower in every generation. He refers to them as '*disciples*', which literally means 'apprentice' or 'learner'.

We all have to choose between two ways of being crazy; the foolishness of the gospel and the nonsense of the values of this world. (Jean Vanier)

Christianity is a statement which, if false, is of no importance, and, if true, of infinite importance. The one thing it cannot be is moderately important. (C.S. Lewis)

He was too great for his disciples . . . He was like some terrible moral huntsman digging mankind out of the snug burrows in which they had lived hitherto . . . Is it any wonder that men were dazzled and blinded and cried out against him? . . . Is it any wonder that to this day this Galilean is too much for our small hearts? (H.G. Wells)

Question

What light does an understanding of apprenticeship shed on the true nature of Christian discipleship? What are the key features of apprenticeship in any trade or profession today?

Bible Study

- **Read Mark 1:16–20, John 15:16, 1 Thessalonians 1:4.** What do these passages tell us about the foundation for Christian discipleship?
- **Read 1 Corinthians 1:26–31.**
  What kind of people does Jesus call to be his disciples? (It may help you to think about the background of the original twelve close followers of Jesus, when answering this question.)
- **Read Luke 6:46–9.**
  What responses does Jesus expect from those who are called to follow him?
    What does it mean practically (rather than theoretically!) to call Jesus 'Lord'? (See quotations on p. 131.)
    What are the areas of your life in which you find it hardest to acknowledge the lordship of Jesus?
    How has God's Word influenced your life in an area that otherwise would not have mattered to you?
- **Read Mark 8:34–8.**
  If you had been with the disciples when Jesus said all this, how might you have reacted?

Deny Yourself

What does it mean to deny self?
    In what area has it been hard for you to deny yourself recently?

Take Up Your Cross . . .

What did it mean for a person literally to take up a cross in Jesus' day?
    What truth about discipleship was Jesus trying to communicate by talking about taking up your cross?
    How can we 'die daily' (see Luke 9:23; 1 Cor. 15:31)?
    Why is it so hard for us to follow this instruction of Jesus?

. . . And Follow Me

Can you think of some other words which mean the same as 'follow'?

In what ways (if any) do you find it easy to imitate Jesus?

In what ways is it difficult to imitate Jesus?

Key verse for memory and meditation: Mark 8:34.

A real Christian is not only a good and well-intentioned person but a man or woman for whom Jesus Christ is ultimately decisive; for whom Jesus – not Caesar, not another god, not money, sex, power, or pleasure – is Lord. (Professor Hans Küng)

By dying like that, Jesus has won the right to be 'our Lord'. The word 'lord' here means 'boss'. This patiently loving master is invited by all Christians into their lives. He enters our lives like a quiet guest. But he stays there to run things if we will let him. Anyone can ask him . . . Anyone can experience his gentle power . . .

There are many ways of defining what 'a Christian' is. The best one is this: a Christian is one who takes orders from Jesus Christ as Lord. (David L. Edwards, former Provost of Southwark Cathedral)

Note: You may wish to read the Summary on p. 24 entitled 'How Can I Become a Disciple?' at this point. (See also p. 129.)

SESSION 2: THE HOLY SPIRIT –
POWER FOR LIVING

In Session 1 we saw that when Jesus calls us, he invites us to become disciples or apprentices. This is a costly business involving the total commitment of our lives to him. Disciples are called by Jesus to serve him and to continue the work on earth which he began two thousand years ago.

But discipleship is a *partnership* with Jesus, for Jesus promises his followers that he will be with them by his Spirit – the Holy Spirit. As the Spirit of Jesus fills our lives, so we are strengthened and empowered to live the kind of life he wants from us – and also to serve him effectively and fruitfully.

Question
In which areas of your life do you feel most in need of God's help? What do you see as your greatest weakness or point of need?

Bible Study
- **Read Ezekiel 36:25–7.**
  What promises does God make to his people? What will the Spirit do for them when he comes to live in their hearts?
- **Read John 14:15–17, 25–6; John 16:5–14.**
  How does Jesus describe the Holy Spirit here? What can we expect him to do in our lives and in the lives of other people?
     Which aspect of the work of the Holy Spirit mentioned here do you find most encouraging/do you most want for yourself?
- **Read Acts 1:5–8.**
  What do you think Jesus means when he talks about being 'baptised in the Holy Spirit'? (Thinking about the way in which John the Baptist administered baptism might help here.)
     How, according to Jesus, will the Holy Spirit help us when he comes upon us?

The Holy Spirit may without exaggeration be called the heartbeat of the Christian, the life-blood of the Christian Church (The Doctrine Commission of the Church of England).

Oscar Peterson is a great jazz pianist. When he was a boy, he was good; very good – and rather bigheaded, too. Then his father bought him a record of Art Tatum, perhaps the finest jazz pianist the world has known. Oscar couldn't believe his ears. 'That's two men playing', he said. But it wasn't. It was one man, with the standard equipment – two hands and ten fingers. Instead of being thrilled at the beautiful playing on the record, Oscar Peterson was so depressed that he didn't play for several weeks, and he had crying fits at night! For he knew that the standard of the pianist on the record seemed way beyond his reach.

Now, when I read the Gospels and hear what Jesus taught, and see how Jesus lived, I sometimes feel like crying and giving up just like Oscar Peterson, for it all seems well beyond my reach. But there is hope, for

- Jesus Christ – Teacher and Lord is also
- Jesus Christ – Saviour, which means helper or rescuer.

He sends his Spirit – the Holy Spirit – into our lives to get to work on our tetchiness, our pettiness, our greed, our gossip, our . . . The Holy Spirit is very practical – and very hands on! He comes into our lives by invitation but he is a restless guest. For the Holy Spirit wants to make us holy and that involves challenge and change as well as comfort and encouragement. (John Young)

- **Read Romans 8:9–17 and 2 Timothy 1:7.**
  What does Paul have to say here about the Holy Spirit and about what he does in the lives of believers?

Can you think of specific ways in which one or more of these great truths has been evident in your own personal experience since you became a Christian?

- **Read Romans 5:5; Romans 8:26–7; Romans 15:13; Philippians 4:11–13; 2 Timothy 1:8.**
  In which specific areas of our Christian lives does the Holy Spirit offer us particular help? How might that help come?

  Can you think of an instance when one of the above verses proved to be true in your own life?

- **Read Isaiah 40:29–31; 2 Corinthians 12:7–10.**
  To whom does God make his promise of power and help?

Key verse for memory and meditation: Philippians 4:13.

For Further Reading
Chapters 2, 3 and 4 of the **Acts of the Apostles** give a graphic account of the change which came over the first disciples when the Holy Spirit first fell upon them. It also gives us some indication of what we might expect him to do in his Church today.

SESSION 3: BE STILL AND KNOW – OPENING UP TO GOD

When we really want to get to know someone, there is no substitute for spending quality time together. The same is true of our relationship with God. Throughout the Gospels we see that Jesus placed a high priority on being alone with his Father. Despite the overwhelming demands on his time, 'Jesus often withdrew to lonely places and prayed' (Luke 5:16). This discipline can be seen in the lives of the great men and women of the Old Testament as well. Moses was one such person.

- **Read Exodus 33:7–11.**
  What do we learn about the nature and content of Moses' quiet times with God? (Note: the cloud was seen by Israel as the visible, outward sign of God's presence with them.)
  What does this teach us about how we might structure our own times of quiet and about what we might expect from them?
  By what means might we expect God to speak to us today?
- **Read Exodus 33:12–23.**
  These verses give us a glimpse into Moses' private dealings with God.
  How would you describe the ways in which Moses communes with God?
  What strikes you particularly about Moses' relationship with God?
  What requests does he make of God?
  How might our meeting with God resemble that of Moses?
- **Read Exodus 34:29–35.**
  How was Moses affected by his time alone with God?
  How were other people affected by Moses' time with God?
  In what ways might we expect our own personal quiet times to have an impact on us and upon other people?

Let's Be Practical . . .

A recent survey by the Bible Society showed that many Christians don't make time in busy lives for daily prayer and Bible reading. Is this a hopeless dream in our modern world?

What are the biggest distractions or hindrances to our spending quality time with the Lord?

How can I overcome these?

What is the best time of day for me to have a regular quiet time?

Which is the most appropriate place for me to have my quiet time?

What topics should I include in my prayers?

Read e.g. **Psalm 9:1–2; Psalm 4:1; Psalm 51:1–2; Psalm 103:1–5; 1 Timothy 2:1–2; Ephesians 6:18–20; Matthew 9:37–8; Matthew 6:9–13; James 5:13–16.**

Key verse for memory and meditation: Exodus 33:11a.

SESSION 4: THE BIBLE – GOD'S WORD FOR ALL TIME

In the previous session we saw that spending time with God is a must if we really want to grow in our relationship with him. We will want to open every area of our lives to God and involve him in all that we do. We shall enlist his help, especially in those areas of life where we encounter difficulties. We will want to talk to him in prayer. But we will, most importantly, want to hear him 'speaking' to us, making his will known to us. Although God communicates with us in a variety of ways (e.g. through the 'inner voice' of the Holy Spirit in our hearts and through the wisdom of other Christians) his primary method of communicating with us – and easily our most reliable source of knowledge of his truth – is the Bible.

- **Read 2 Timothy 3:15–17.**
  What makes the Bible different from any other literature or teachings/opinions?

  What, according to Paul, is the Bible useful for?

  Can you think of any specific ways in which your own experience has proved the truth of what Paul teaches here?
- **Read Romans 15:4, Acts 20:32 and Psalm 119:9–11, 105.**
  For what purposes are the Scriptures given to us?
- **Read Psalm 19:7–11.**
  Which words does the Psalmist use to describe the nature of God's Word?

  What benefits does he suggest come from reading God's Word?

  How does this Psalm affect the way we might think of the Bible?
- **Read Mark 4:13–20.**
  What common hindrances to the effective receiving of God's

Word does Jesus spell out here?

Can you think of ways in which these, or other similar obstacles to receiving God's Word, might gain a hold in your own life?

A Practical Approach to Getting the Most out of the Bible . . .

There are four different aspects to our approach to the Bible:

1 **Reading Scripture**
   Read Deuteronomy 17:18–20.
   How would you advise a new Christian to begin to set about reading the Bible?

2 **Studying Scripture**
   Read Joshua 1:8, Psalm 1:1–3.
   What does it mean to *study* God's Word, and what are the benefits of such study?

3 **Memorising Scripture**
   Read Psalm 40:8, Psalm 119:9–11.

During his long years in captivity and solitary confinement, Terry Waite was sustained by the fact that he had memorised large sections of the Book of Common Prayer, the Psalms and other Bible passages.

---

4 **Meditating upon Scripture**
   Read Psalm 119:27, Colossians 3:16. (See also the paragraph by David L. Edwards on p. 116.)

   What new, practical steps am I going to take in my own personal approach to studying the Bible as a result of what I have learned through this course?

Key verse for memory and meditation: Psalm 119:105.

SESSION 5: THE CHURCH – GOD'S NEW PEOPLE

Many people today seem to regard the Church as something of an optional extra to real Christianity. 'You don't have to go to church to be a Christian' is a common refrain. There is an element of truth in this. Certainly the act of 'going to church' doesn't make you a Christian or affect your *standing* with God in any way whatsoever. But it does affect your *relationship* with God and with God's people. It is almost impossible to grow as a Christian if you do not

- join in fellowship with other members of the Christian family
- share with others in weekly, public worship
- receive the teaching from God's Word which is a vital element in every worship service.

The Bible has no understanding whatsoever of the Christian life as a solitary activity. The commonest New Testament word to describe a Christian is the word 'Saint': it *never* occurs in the singular but *always* in the plural. The Church lies at the centre of God's plans for the world, and every individual Christian has a vital role to play in its life. For this reason the writer of the letter to the Hebrews (10:25) reminds us: 'Let us not give up meeting together, as some are in the habit of doing, but let us encourage one another.'

- **Read 1 Peter 2:9–10.**
  Peter uses several different images to describe the Church. What do they teach us about the nature, purpose and task of the Church?
- **Read Ephesians 5:25, Colossians 1:18.**
  What do we learn here about Jesus' attitude towards, and relationship with, the Church – *his* Church?

How does this affect the way we see our own place within the Church?

- **Read Romans 12:4–5, 1 Corinthians 12:12, 25–7.**
  What do these verses teach us about the life of the Church, and about our place within it?

  Can you think of a time when one of these truths was especially borne out in your own experience? How?

- **Read Ephesians 4:11–16.**
  What are God's aims and intentions for the Church?

  What has he done to ensure that these goals are achieved?

  What must we do in order to co-operate with God's purposes?

  Paul talks of every part of the body doing its work (verse 16).

  What specific work has God called you to do at the present time?

- **Read Acts 2:42–7.**
  What were the essential elements of life in the early Church?

  In which of these areas is the life of your own church particularly strong/weak?

- What, according to the following verses, are our responsibilities as members of the body of Christ? **John 13:34; Romans 14:13; Romans 15:7; 1 Corinthians 1:10; Galatians 5:13; Galatians 6:1–2; Ephesians 4:32; Colossians 3:9; Hebrews 10:25; Hebrews 13:17; James 5:16; 1 Peter 4:8–10.**

  What action must we take to put these instructions into practice?

Key verse for memory and meditation: 1 Corinthians 12:27.

SESSION 6: PERSONAL HOLINESS –
IMITATING GOD

To follow Jesus means to imitate him and to take our lead from him in every area of our lives. This would be impossible if we were called to achieve this through our own natural strength and ability. The good news is that what is humanly *im*possible, God has put within our grasp by his goodness and grace. If we are Christians, then the Bible tells us that God helps us to put to death our old nature and gives us a new nature, the nature of Jesus himself. Imitating Jesus is simply (!) a question of allowing our new nature to show through in every area of our lives, and making sure that our old nature is not allowed to raise its ugly head ever again. We all know that this is a huge struggle but a glorious one, and one which we undertake in God's strength.

In this session we explore something of what is involved in personal holiness, of being distinctive and different for God's sake. We shall apply these lessons to one key area of life in which, perhaps, we encounter most difficulty when it comes to living the new life – the use of our tongues!

(Note: *For a fine definition of holiness by Cardinal Basil Hume, see p. 105.*)

- **Read Ephesians 4:17–24.**
  What instructions does Paul give us here about living the new life in Christ? In practical terms, what does it mean to follow these instructions?

  How does Paul describe our 'new self'? (See also Colossians 1:21–2.)
- **Read James 3:3–12.**
  What insights are we given here into language and the way we should use our tongues?

What do you find most challenging in these words?

- **Read Ephesians 4:25–5:4.**
  Notice how much of Paul's teaching concerning personal holiness refers to our words and speaking. What specific instructions are we given about the use of our tongues? What instructions do we find most pertinent to ourselves and our own situations? How can we strive to apply them more effectively?

- What other warnings about our use of words do we find in the following verses: **Matthew 12:33–7; James 1:26; James 4:11?**

- The following verses give positive encouragement to use our speech wisely for the benefit of others and for the glory of God: **Psalm 34:1; Psalm 45:1; Proverbs 15:1–4; Isaiah 50:4; Colossians 4:5, 6.**

  What lessons do we learn from these, and how can we apply these lessons in practical terms to our own lives?

The most dangerous proverb in the entire English language must be the old saying that 'there's no smoke without fire'. This gives credibility to every malicious rumour-monger. One man's entire career was ruined by an accusation that has no foundation in fact. No wonder the ninth commandment tells us not to bear false witness. To steal a person's reputation is worse than taking their handbag or wallet.

Psalm 141:3 (GNB) is a useful prayer to use at the beginning of each day, or at times when we find it difficult to control our tongues:

Lord, place a guard at my mouth, a sentry at the door of my lips.

Key verse for memory and meditation: Ephesians 4:29.

SESSION 7: GUIDANCE – KNOWING GOD'S WILL FOR MY LIFE

One area about which there is a great deal of confusion is this tricky matter of 'guidance'. In our better moments we want to serve and please God in all things; we long to know what precisely he expects from us in each and every situation. But so often we feel ignorant of his will for us and deep down we feel that perhaps we are not following his will as we ought. Worse still, we half-expect God to hold us responsible for not discerning his will properly.

Actually, nowhere in the Bible does God promise to give us 'guidance' as a kind of impersonal commodity. What he does promise – frequently – is that *he himself will be our guide* as we live our daily lives. He promises to guide us in a variety of ways, sometimes without our even realising it.

In this session we shall seek to uncover some of the most common ways in which God does guide us and learn how we might more effectively co-operate with him as he seeks to lead us. Before starting on the Bible study, you might enjoy the Questionnaire. Jot down your answers and share your findings. (*Note: pp. 68–72 also relates to this topic.*)

Questionnaire – Making Decisions
1 Do you believe that God guides in the big decisions of life?
2 Do you believe that God guides in the small details of life?
3 Do you believe that God promises guidance to:
  (a) all people?
  (b) all Christians?
  (c) obedient Christians?

(d) full-time Christian workers?

4 Does God guide by signs? (a) Always?
                          (b) Never?
                          (c) Sometimes?
                          (d) Usually?

5 Is guidance mainly a question of   (a) feeling?
                                     (b) thinking?

6 Does our common sense play   (a) some part?
                               (b) a large part?
                               (c) no part?

7 When faced with an important decision do you
   (a) pray about it?
   (b) ask a friend to pray about it?
   (c) ask a friend for advice about it?
   (d) ask the advice of your family?
   (e) ask an older Christian for advice?

8 When choosing a job, money is
   (a) sometimes a factor?
   (b) never a factor?
   (c) always one of the main factors?

9 Which prayer for guidance do you prefer?
   (a) O Lord, give me faith to believe that you will guide
   me when I make this decision.
   (b) O Lord, give me a sign, so that I may be certain I am
   making the right decision.

10 When seeking guidance from God do you look for a
   specific verse in the Bible to help you
   (a) Sometimes?
   (b) Never?
   (c) Always?

11 (a) A new Christian asks your advice about Bible passages
   relating to issues of guidance and finding and doing God's
   will. Could you produce a couple of passages?
   (b) Why are Romans 8:28 and Psalm 25:8–9 so
   encouraging?

12 Can you recall an occasion when your faith has helped
   with, or caused problems over, a decision?

- **Read Isaiah 48:17, Psalm 32:8 and Psalm 23:3.**
   What does God promise his people in these verses?
- In what different ways, according to the following verses, does
   God guide us? How might we describe the manner in which
   God guides us in these different ways, and can you think of
   some specific occasions when you have experienced God
   guiding you in such ways?
   **Psalm 119:11, Psalm 119:105, 2 Timothy 3:16–17;
   Romans 8:14; 1 Corinthians 2:12; Proverbs 12:15; Acts
   15:5–7.**

The Bible records many instances when God seems to act in
a very dramatic way to make his will known. But these are
exceptional situations when God is communicating very
specific information which simply could not be discovered
from the exercise of holy common sense, or from taking
good advice from other people. And of course, unlike us,
people in Bible times could not take a Bible from the book-
shelf! Scrolls belonged to communities rather than individuals.

- The following verses show how God guided the early Church
   from time to time and, indeed, how he still chooses to guide his
   people on occasions today. What methods of guidance does he
   use in the following passages, and why do you think he chose
   such methods? **Acts 13:1–3; Acts 16:6–10; Acts 18:9–11.**
   Do you have any personal experience of God guiding you or
   others in these or other ways?
- Can you think of other ways in which God guides people today?
- What, according to the following verses, must we do in order
   to know and understand God's will? **Psalm 32:9; Proverbs**

3:5–7; Romans 12:1–2; James 1:5–7.
- What is the most important thing you have learned from this session, and what action are you going to take because of this study?

Key verse for memory and meditation: Psalm 32:8.

SESSION 8: TEMPTATION AND VICTORY – THE NEVER-ENDING STRUGGLE

The apostle Paul tells us (Col. 1:13) that, as Christians, we have been rescued from the domain of darkness and *transferred* to the Kingdom of God's Son. In other words, we have swapped sides and changed our loyalties. From now on, though, we find ourselves involved in a struggle. It is a spiritual battle, in which our former master seeks to knock us off course, to undermine and disrupt our progress in the Christian life.

We all know the reality of this struggle and we often feel that we are losing the battle. We can take heart, however, from the fact that our adversary, Satan, was comprehensively defeated by the death and resurrection of Jesus, and his days are numbered. He does have limited power to disrupt, but he can never completely frustrate God's purposes. Further, God has put the Spirit of his Son into our hearts to strengthen and equip us for every eventuality. Although the struggle will never cease this side of eternity, we need not be defeated by it.

In what ways, or in which areas of our lives, do we find ourselves most prone to temptation or other threat to our Christian discipleship?

- What do the following verses teach us about the nature and origin of temptation: **1 John 2:15–17; James 1:12–14; Ephesians 6:10–13; Luke 4:1–13?**

    In what ways was Jesus tempted here?

    What similarities do we find here between Jesus' experience and our own experience of temptation?

    What do we learn from the way in which Jesus dealt with the attacks of the devil here?
- What other instructions concerning temptation and how to counter it, are we given in Scripture? **Ephesians 6:10–13;**

Ephesians 4:27; James 4:7.
- What encouragement do the following verses give us as we struggle with temptation: **2 Thessalonians 3:3; Hebrews 2:18, 4:15–16?**

Key verse for memory and meditation: Ephesians 6:11.

SESSION 9: MONEY, TIME AND TALENTS –
GENEROUS TOWARDS GOD

God is a wonderfully generous Father who showers his love upon us in a carefree and unfettered way. He longs for us to reflect his love and generosity – not only towards him but also in our relationships with one another. Love makes demands upon us and all our resources. To call Jesus 'Lord' means to put all that we have at his full disposal. John Stott corrected our usual perspective when he said, 'It's not a question of how much of *my* money do I give to God, but how much of *God's* money do I keep for myself.' (*Note: The session which starts on p. 10 also deals with this subject.*)

- **Read 1 Chronicles 29:10–16.**
  What different resources do we have at our disposal?
      How can we use them for the service of God and for the benefit of others?
      What kind of an attitude should we have towards these resources, according to King David?
      Which of our own resources/possessions do we find it most difficult to regard as belonging to God?
- **Read Matthew 6:19–21 and 24–34.**
  What does it mean to 'store up treasures in heaven' (v. 20)?
      What other warnings and instructions are we given here concerning our attitudes to riches and resources?
- **Read 2 Corinthians 8:1–9.**
  What lessons do we learn from the Macedonian Christians, and what might it mean for us to apply these lessons to ourselves?

Many Christians have found a planned approach to giving to be both practical and biblical. Planning ensures against irregular or unwise giving, and also against neglect. In an age when there are so many demands upon our time and money, planned giving helps us honour the Lord with what we have.

A good plan will include these steps:

1   Thoughtfully decide what percentage of your income you will return to the Lord – a minimum percentage.
2   Set aside the Lord's portion first whenever you receive money. Put this aside to be used as he leads. Once set aside it is his and should not be used for any other purpose.
3   Prayerfully distribute the Lord's money as he directs: it is usually best to do this at a regular time – weekly or monthly.

Make extra gifts and adjust your giving as God increases your faith and as your own financial situation changes (of course, you may need to give less, if your income reduces).

Those who dedicate their resources to God are dedicating themselves. To fail to do so is not to commit oneself fully to God.

- **Read Matthew 25:14–30.**
  What 'talents' do you have? The way we use our God-given abilities and time is even more important than the way we use our money.

  What is the most important lesson you have learned in this session?

  What action are you going to take as a result?

Key verse for memory and meditation: Matthew 6:21.

To accept Jesus because he is the Truth involves a revolution in our behaviour and moral standards, and in our entire outlook on life – for he comes with tough demands.

He comes too, with unutterable comfort. To a world beset by problems he comes as guide. In a world where many are lonely, he comes as friend. To a world which often seems to lack meaning, he brings understanding. For a world tempted to despair, he provides the ground of hope. Over a world where dying is the single certainty, he sits enthroned as the conqueror of death.

The words of Jesus, as recorded by St John, have been tested and proved in the lives of countless thousands of men and women: 'I am the light of the world. Whoever follows me will never walk in darkness, but will have the light of life' (John 8:12).

(John Young)

Good News is for Sharing

SESSION 1: HERE AM I . . . SEND SOMEBODY ELSE!

A Course on Evangelism *by the Revd Ian Parkinson, Vicar of Saltburn in North Yorkshire. Ian is an experienced pastor and a fine evangelist, with wide experience of devising and leading courses for groups (see Preface). He wishes to record his indebtedness to Scripture Union, whose course, entitled* Care To Say Something, *sparked many of the ideas in this course.*

> There is an audio-tape which accompanies this course, available from York Courses (for address see p. x). Unlike the first four courses, however, the cassette is not an integral part of the course but acts as a supplement to it. The tape consists of interviews with leading figures in the world of evangelism, including the Revd Brian Hoare, the Revd Robin Gamble, Bishop Gavin Reid and Canon Robert Warren.

The Church is the only organisation which exists for the benefit of those who are not its members. (Archbishop William Temple)

The Church exists by mission as fire exists by burning. (Professor Emil Brunner)

It seems to me that any church which does not see evangelism and outreach as its primary aim is not doing the work it was created to do. (Bishop Gordon Bates)

We must never forget that the renewal and release of the laity, through the parish clergy, is the key to evangelism. (1988 Lambeth Conference of Anglican Bishops)

Evangelism is not primarily about holding special missions and evangelistic events – though at times they may be appropriate. It is about something far deeper and more subtle; nothing less than changing the order of priorities of many of our congregations. (Bishop Nigel McCulloch)

Isaiah did *not* say, 'how aggressive or assertive are the feet that bring the gospel of peace'. He wrote, 'how *beautiful* . . .' Evangelism is any activity or encounter which causes someone to hear about Jesus or his Church and think, 'That's good' or 'I'd like to hear more'. (John Young)

Although evangelism is the most pressing and urgent responsibility which faces the Christian Church, it is a word which often drives us to a sense of:

- *fear* because we lack confidence to share our faith,
- *guilt* because we tend to avoid doing so,
- *failure* because we rarely see our own friends come to faith, and
- *embarrassment* because evangelism is caricatured as intruding uninvited into other people's lives.

> The biggest problem in evangelism is not to find methods but to *motivate* people; it would be futile to suppose that Christians do not evangelise because they don't know what to do. It is not ignorance but motivation which is the trouble. There is not enough fire in the belly. Once the fire is there people discover methods – where there is a will there is always a way! (Michael Green)

Seven Powerful Motives for Getting on with the Task of Evangelism
(See p. 86 for a slightly different list.)

1 *The love of God*
   - God cares so much for the world and is so concerned for its salvation that he sent his son to die (John 3:16).
   - Paul spoke of this same love driving him on in his own service and witness (2 Cor. 5:14).

2 *The command of Jesus Christ*
   Jesus' last instruction to his disciples before he left earth was that they were to carry on the work he had started.

   Then Jesus came to them and said, 'All authority in heaven and on earth has been given to me. Therefore go and make disciples of all nations, baptising them in the name of the Father and of the Son and of the Holy Spirit, and teaching them to obey everything I have commanded you. And surely I am with you always, to the very end of the age.' (Matt. 28:18–20)

3 *The thrust of the Holy Spirit*
   John 14 and 16 speak of the Holy Spirit as the 'Comforter' in the older versions of the Bible. The word 'comfort' did not mean to console or lend a shoulder to cry on, but 'to spur on into action'. This connects with Acts 1:8 (note the link between the Holy Spirit and witnessing).

4 *The needs of other people*
   The Bible tells us that those without Christ are spiritually dead (Eph. 2:1); far from God's saving presence (Rom. 3:23); powerless to please God (Rom. 8:8). We are guardians and stewards of the good news which can change all that for them.

5 *A sense of responsibility*
   Paul speaks of himself as an 'Ambassador for Christ' (2 Cor. 5:20). An ambassador is someone who represents and speaks on behalf of a sovereign or state leader, in a foreign country. If the ambassador does not speak up, his or her country's interests cannot be known. 'How can people call [on God] for help if

they have not believed? And how can they believe if they have not heard the message? And how can they hear if the message is not proclaimed?' (Rom. 10:14, GNB).

6 *A sense of privilege*

We have the great privilege of having been brought from sin to salvation, from spiritual death to eternal life, from being far from God to being reconciled to him, and also of being called to serve him, the King of Kings. Having heard and received the 'glad tidings of great joy', should we not pass them on?

7 *Evangelism brings joy*

We know that there is joy in heaven over one sinner who repents (Luke 15:7). We know too that coming to faith in Christ brought joy to us. Equally, there can be few things which cause us to feel happier than seeing a friend come to faith in Christ – nothing spurs us on quite so much in our enthusiasm for God's work.

First Workshop

Read through the following statements slowly and thoughtfully. Tick no more than three which you feel best describe your own position. If you have other feelings or fears then write them down.

'I am reluctant to talk about Christianity because . . .'

(a) I am afraid I will offend others.
(b) I really don't know what to say.
(c) I feel that it isn't my job to talk to others about Christ.
(d) I don't have much contact with people who are not Christians.
(e) I don't think I have the answers to questions people might ask.
(f) I don't think my relationship with God is strong enough.
(g) Though I do have faith in God, I seldom experience his power and influence in my life.
(h) I am afraid of being rejected or laughed at.
(i) People will think I am a hypocrite.
(j) I wouldn't know how to begin a conversation about Jesus.
(k) I would be embarrassed.
(l) I am just not motivated enough to share my faith.
(m) I don't like setting myself up as an expert.

(n) I don't think other people would be interested in what I have to say.
(o) I believe Christianity is a private matter and not something to be talked about.
(p) My non-Christian friends seem happy enough without Jesus.
(q)   ⎱ add your
(r)   ⎰ own
(s)   comments
(t)   here

Most of the problems we have in sharing our faith fall into one of three categories:

(a) Problems relating to ourselves, e.g. 'I'm afraid of being embarrassed.'
(b) Problems relating to others, e.g. 'I'm afraid of causing offence.'
(c) Problems relating to the message, e.g. 'I haven't got the answers people require.'

Which (if any) looms largest for you?

The Most Effective Evangelism Ever Invented

David Watson, one of the finest evangelists of the twentieth century, wrote the following: 'It is important to stress that not every Christian is called to be an evangelist. All are witnesses to Christ; all must be committed to the Church's task of evangelism; but only some are evangelists.'

Many people in our churches feel unable to talk intelligently about God, prayer, Jesus, sin and eternal life. But they can witness to their faith – as the following true stories by John Young show.

- *First example* As a student I was invited to a Christian weekend. The student who invited me didn't talk about his faith in any detail. He simply explained what would happen at the residential weekend and said, 'I'm going, it's going to be good. Will you come with me?' I accepted his invitation and heard a convincing speaker (Donald English) expound the Christian faith. Seeds were sown, which came to fruition in my own life.

- *Second example* A few years ago I received a phone call from a pastor in Cambridge. 'Thank you,' he said, 'for inviting me to that meeting all those years ago when we were students.' (I had completely forgotten that I did invite him!) The same thing had happened to him. Seeds of faith were sown and God's Spirit caused these to grow. I had been nothing more than a witness. I hadn't explained the Gospel; I had simply invited him to join me.

(On p. 145 John explains why he believes that *witnesses* are even more important than evangelists.)

Second Workshop
1 Draw up a list of events in your church to which you might invite people – social events as well as services.
2 Each person draw up a list of three people for whom they will pray and to whom they will offer an invitation.
3 Design an invitation card for one of these events.

Finally . . .
Professor Robin Gill suggests that 'Belonging precedes believing'. It is as people experience Christian friendship, fellowship and love that they become open to Christian truth. This is rooted in the Bible. Look up John 1:40–6 for a Bible story which illustrates the power of a simple invitation.

In closing, read this passage together, keep silence and close with the Grace.

SESSION 2: AND NOW FOR THE GOOD NEWS!

To evangelise is to present Christ Jesus to sinful men in order that, through the power of the Holy Spirit, they may come to put their trust in God through him. (Dr J. I. Packer)

Evangelism is the presentation of the claims of Christ, in the power of the Spirit, to a world in need, by a Church in love. (Grove Booklet – *A New Canterbury Tale*)

Five Key Points about the True Nature of Evangelism

1 *Presenting a person*

Evangelism is all about introducing people to a person, Jesus Christ, and his relevance and availability. It is not a question of trying to persuade people to accept a new philosophy or creed or way of life. Evangelism is letting people know about our best friend.

2 *A world in need*

We live in an age of almost unparalleled ignorance concerning Christian truth, yet also an age of great spiritual hunger and openness. There has never, in our lifetimes, been a time of greater opportunity to present the Christian good news. Yet we cannot simply 'let people come to their own conclusions about spiritual matters' and treat these as essentially private affairs. Many people are locked in complete ignorance about God and his love revealed in Jesus Christ. Our task is one of *education* as much as *persuasion*.

   We are those who have discovered that which many others crave (albeit unconsciously). We cannot, selfishly, keep this to ourselves. 'Evangelism is one beggar telling another beggar where he found bread!' (D.T. Niles). One new Christian spoke of her friend as a 'bridge' to faith in God – a lovely description.

3 *A partnership with God*

We often feel rather alone and weak when we think of, or engage in, sharing our faith. But evangelism is something we do in partnership with God – it is a joint effort.
- Paul speaks of being co-workers with God (2 Cor. 6:1).
- Jesus tells his disciples that he will always be with them in their service of him (Matt. 28:20).
- It was the Holy Spirit who worked with Paul as he preached to the Thessalonian churches (1 Thess. 1:5).

It doesn't depend upon how 'good' we are at sharing our faith!

'Evangelism means to carry Jesus in your heart and to give the presence of Jesus to someone else' (attributed to Mother Teresa).

4 *Responsibility of all*
It is the work of the whole Church without exception. In the early Church the Gospel was passed on primarily by the 'ordinary' people, the 'idiots' (literally that, in the Greek!).

An evangelist winning 1,000 people for Christ every night of every year would take more than 10,000 years to win the whole world, ignoring the population explosion. If one individual Christian disciple were to win one new person each year and train that new Christian to do the same, the entire world would be won for Christ in . . . 32 years. (Dr James Kennedy)

'Always be prepared to answer anyone who asks you to explain the hope you have within you' (1 Pet. 3:15, GNB). Being an effective and prepared witness simply means . . . 'being able to interpret our experience and assurance in the light of the revealed truths of the Gospel' (Eddie Gibbs).

5 *A process rather than a single event*
The average length of time it takes someone to come to clear faith and commitment is *four years* after first being exposed to the Gospel message. We need to see our witness as just one link in a long chain. It is helpful to look back over our own

experience and reflect on the many different influences which played a part at different times in our coming to faith and growing in faith.

Workshop Session
In groups of four or five look at the definitions of 'evangelism' on pp. 142, 147.

(a) Are there any definitions which are completely wrong? Why are they wrong?
(b) Pick your top three definitions of 'evangelism' and put them into some order of priority.
(c) Can you think of a better definition of evangelism – one which might shed further light on the task in hand for the Church?
(d) Other definitions of evangelism are scattered throughout this book (e.g. pp. 184–5, 190).

EVANGELISM IS OFFERING OURSELVES TO OTHERS IN DEEDS, NOT JUST WORDS	EVANGELISM IS NOT PREACHING CHRISTIANITY BUT OFFERING CHRIST	EVANGELISM IS TALKING ABOUT GOD USING A SET FORMULA WITH PRESCRIBED SLOGANS
EVANGELISM IS SHARING JESUS CHRIST	EVANGELISM IS TO HELP PEOPLE INTO A MORE HARMONIOUS RELATIONSHIP WITH OTHERS	EVANGELISM MEANS MISSIONS AND CAMPAIGNS TO FILL THE CHURCHES
EVANGELISM IS FORCING RELIGION DOWN PEOPLE'S THROATS	EVANGELISM IS GOSSIPING THE GOSPEL TO OUR NEIGHBOUR	EVANGELISM MEANS EXPLAINING THAT THE LIFE, DEATH AND RESURRECTION OF JESUS IS GOOD NEWS FROM GOD
EVANGELISM IS TELLING PEOPLE THAT THEY ARE SINNERS	EVANGELISM MEANS WITNESSING TO CHRIST IN WORD AND ACTION	EVANGELISM IS JUST BEING THERE AS A CHRISTIAN IN THE COMMUNITY
EVANGELISM MEANS LEADING SOMEONE TO A COMMITMENT TO JESUS CHRIST	EVANGELISM IS STANDING ON A STREET CORNER SHOUTING, 'REPENT, FOR THE DAY, OF JUDGEMENT IS NEAR'	EVANGELISM IS FILLING OUR PEWS IN ORDER TO BOOST OUR CHURCH FINANCES

SESSION 3: OWNING UP!

You will not find many exhortations to evangelism in the New Testament. For the most part the writers simply assume that the Gospel is being shared and that people are coming to faith. The first-century churches had many problems, but stagnation in evangelism was not one of them. (Dr Stephen Travis)

What we need to do is to rediscover the uncomplicated, unembarrassed style of witness of the early believers so that witnessing becomes almost as natural as breathing. (John Allan)

The outside world may never come to church to hear a sermon, but the outside world sees us every day and our lives must be the sermon to them of new life in Christ. (Professor William Barclay)

Our experience of faith is often of interest and, indeed, of help to others. It is important that we are able, in some way, to put this into words. In the first century the good news about Jesus spread rapidly because ordinary people told their friends and neighbours about this remarkable man and the impact he had made upon their lives.

Luke 4:14, 4:37	The news about Jesus spread like wildfire
Luke 5:25	The paralytic glorified God for what he had done for him
Luke 5:29	Levi brought his friends to meet Jesus
Luke 8:38–9	Jesus instructed the demoniac to return home and witness to God's activity in his life

Luke 13:13	The healed woman glorified God for what he had done
Luke 18:43	Blind Bartimaeus began to follow Jesus and others joined in praise of God as a result of his testimony
Luke 24:9	The women reported the resurrection to others
Luke 24:44–8	Jesus instructed his followers to be *witnesses* to him

---

Each person has a different experience. St Paul had a dramatic experience and a spectacular meeting with Jesus (Acts 26:9–22). But some people, especially those with Christian parents or a long association with the church, find that their relationship with Jesus grows gradually; they can't always point to the day or the time when they became Christians. That doesn't matter, the important thing is to be able to speak about an experience that is real and meaningful in the details of everyday life now, rather than some spectacular event in the past. (from *Care to Say Something*, Scripture Union)

(See also p. 151 for helpful comments from a former Provost of Southwark Cathedral.)

Workshop
First Task

We are now going to make an attempt at putting our own experience of faith into words. Look back over your own experience. When did you first become aware of God's reality? When has your faith been *most* alive and meaningful? What experiences, events and people have been especially significant for you in terms of your journey of faith and relationship with God? Filling in two or three of the dotted lines may help to clarify the details of your spiritual pilgrimage.

Significant dates ....

Significant events ....

Significant organisations ....
Significant experiences ....
Significant people ....

When sharing your own faith story:
- Be completely honest; don't exaggerate, even to bring 'extra credit' to God!
- Don't be afraid of mentioning things which might appear strange – or mundane;
- Do bring the story up to date to show that your relationship with God is not tied to just one or two past events but is still growing;
- Don't drag things out or pad out the story with unnecessary details.

Second Task

Now get into threes. In this section you will find out from the two others how God has become real to them over the years – not just the dramatic events but also those less spectacular times when God has had something to teach them.

Each member of the trio has four or five minutes to tell his or her story of faith. You may ask questions just like an interviewer if it helps, and some suggested questions are given below.

1   Have there been any special occasions in your life when God has been particularly real or close to you? Give details.
2   What things about God or God's people have made a particular impression upon you?
3   Was there any time that you can identify when you first realised that you had faith in Jesus or wanted to have such faith? If so, give details.
4   What does your faith mean to you in ordinary, everyday living?

Third Task

Are you willing to pray during the next week that you will get an opportunity to share something from your 'faith-story' with people whom you know?

In Closing . . .

Turn to pp. 24 and 129 and read one of the Summaries, using several voices.

SESSION 4: THE GOSPEL CONNECTION

One of the factors which most hinders us in our witness and evangelism is that, deep down, we sometimes wonder if the Christian faith really is relevant to our friends who are not yet Christians. So often, on the surface, people seem quite happy without Jesus Christ playing any significant part in their lives. They seem content to treat God rather as a pilot treats his parachute: glad that it is there in the background, but rather hoping he'll never have to use it!

Those outside the Church sometimes talk of the Christian faith as being old-fashioned, out of date, an interesting museum piece but of no real use today without profound modification.

However, when we begin to examine more deeply the felt needs of people around us, we begin to see that many people, under the surface, are not really quite so 'complete' as they may at first seem. They sometimes admit, rather wistfully, that they would like to have a living faith. Further, when we look at Jesus Christ, we find that he claims to be able to meet precisely those needs which are at the top of people's agendas in our modern world.

Workshop

Stage 1

> The hopes and fears of all the years
> Are met in thee tonight.
> (from 'O Little Town of Bethlehem')

Jot down some answers to the following questions:

(a) What three things do most people most want out of life?
(b) What three things do people most fear?

(c) What three things do people sense to be most lacking in their lives today?

(d) In your view, is it true that many people 'live lives of quiet desperation'?

(e) Allow five minutes for jotting, then get into fours to share your answers.

Stage 2

In these groups of four, consider the following:

Some people seem to have few if any unmet needs and appear to be quite happy without Jesus Christ. But Jesus himself tells us of needs we all have even though we might not realise this. In your groups, read the following verses together. What do these verses teach us about the spiritual needs which are common to all people, and about the spiritual predicament of each and every one of us?

- Ephesians 2:1–3
- John 8:34–6
- Isaiah 59:2
- Romans 3:23

Stage 3

We look next at some of the things Jesus had to say to the people of his own day, and specifically at the way in which he addressed their spiritual needs. How, according to these verses, does Jesus 'fill the gap' which so many people experience in their lives? Do we learn anything here of *how* we might begin to pass on the Christian good news to others and of *what* we might say to them?

- Matthew 11:28
- John 7:37–9
- Mark 2:5–12
- John 8:12
- John 3:16–18
- John 8:36
- John 4:10–14
- John 10:10
- John 6:35
- John 14:5–6

Stage 4
Finally, in your groups, think of the following people:

1   An old lady who lives alone, and who equates Christianity with being British, and with doing good to others, and who has always 'tried her best'.
2   A young couple who have just had their first baby. They have no Christian background but are amazed at the wonder of their new arrival and feel nervous about coping with the enormous responsibilities of parenthood.
3   An unemployed man with a teenage family. He has no hope of another job and is beginning to feel useless, frustrated and rejected.
4   A man who is happily married with a young family, a good job at which he is very successful, and with excellent prospects. Outwardly he seems to have everything.
5   A parent whose teenage child has just died in tragic circumstances.

Pick out one or two of the situations above. In your groups discuss these questions about the people you have chosen:

(a)   What might be the particular spiritual needs of these people?
(b)   What might Jesus say to them if he met them today?
(c)   How might we listen effectively to them (see Course 8 and p. 73)?
(d)   How might we present the Gospel to them, so that they might hear it *as* good news?
(e)   Think back over the previous weeks. Is there anything in our own stories of faith which might be helpful to any of the above people or situations?
(f)   Consider all this in the light of Bishop John Finney's assertion that 'evangelism is helping people to belong so that they can believe'.

SESSION 5: LOOKING OUT FOR THE CHURCH

When the Church of Jesus Christ is the sort of Church that Jesus intended it to be, it will automatically and inevitably be an evangelistic Church. For the Church is intended to be an incarnate presence of Jesus Christ; saying the things he says, doing the things he does, and by the power of the Holy Spirit being the sort of Church that continually makes Jesus Christ present in our world today. The primary task, therefore . . . is to energise that Church and so help it to become what it is truly intended to be. (Bishop Michael Marshall)

Compared to evangelism, so much of what has taken place in the Church in recent years has been rather like re-arranging the furniture whilst the house is on fire! (David Watson)

There is both an individual and a corporate dimension to evangelism. God addresses us personally and individually, and this must be reflected in our own witness. However, there is a strong 'together' aspect to all this – the Church is called to be an evangelistic organisation. We need to understand how we might effectively order the life of our churches so as to facilitate this basic task. This will have repercussions for our church structures and also for our churches' attitudes to the outsider as well as to church members.

The principal challenge to all churches is how far we are prepared to abandon the prevailing 'maintenance mentality' which has gripped our churches for so long and led to an over-concentration on internal church and/or domestic matters. Replacing this with a 'mission mentality' will be scary but exciting!

It is instructive to examine the attitudes of the very earliest churches. They have a good deal to teach us about priorities for church life and about recovering evangelistic zeal. These churches were by no means perfect. They got a lot of things wrong (many of the New Testament letters were written for this very reason). So they do not provide an exact blue-print for church order and life today. But in this foremost matter of evangelism they leave us standing.

Workshop
Stage 1
Read the following Bible passages and try to identify significant features in the life of the early Church which led to the remarkable evangelistic impact of that Church.

- Acts 2:42–7
- Acts 4:23–31
- Acts 6:1–4
- 1 Thessalonians 1:1–10 (the example of the Thessalonian Christians)
- 1 Thessalonians 2:1–12 (the example of the ministry of Paul and Silas)
    - Which features of the early Church do we recognise as being present in our own churches today?
    - Which features are most clearly lacking? How can we work to ensure that we recapture these necessary emphases in our own day and age?
    - Are there differences in our cultural setting (e.g. are we in a post-Christian, secular setting?) which make our task more difficult than theirs?

The task of evangelism for the Church has several different facets:
- At the most basic level it involves making contact with those outside the family of the Church. Growing churches have a 'presence' in the community. They *are* 'good news' – making links with other organisations and providing valuable services (mums and toddlers groups, lunch clubs, etc.). They form a bridge between Jesus and the modern world.

- Second, it involves providing a context in which the Christian Gospel can be explained in a relevant and accessible manner. A vital part of evangelism in this generation is basic education, the straightforward communication of information about the person and significance of Jesus Christ to a society which is by and large ignorant of such truths. Groups for hospitality, teaching and discussion are invaluable (e.g. an Alpha course, the Emmaus course or the course you are on right now!).
- Third, and arising out of the above, evangelism involves 'apologetics'. This means providing a defence or justification of the *truth* of the Christian faith. It involves giving an account of the Christian answer to such questions as 'Why does God allow suffering?', 'Do all religions lead to God?', 'Hasn't science disproved God's existence?' as well as highlighting the inadequacies of other rival world views, e.g. New Age spirituality. (See Booklist on p. ii.)
- Fourth, evangelism involves giving people opportunities to make a response of faith and commitment to the challenge of Jesus Christ. The goal of evangelism is to draw people into Christian discipleship.
- Finally, the evangelistic task involves the careful nurture of new believers, helping them to grow in faith, understanding and Christian character.

Stage 2

In your groups, discuss how your own churches can ensure that all the above elements of the evangelistic task are adequately covered. How are we currently providing for these tasks to be discharged? What more could we do to discharge them more effectively?

Human story touches human story in the midst of God's story (Statement by the Anglican Primates).

An *evangelist* needs to be articulate about the Christian faith. He or she will be well able to handle 'God's story' in the Bible and in history.

A *witness* does not need to be articulate about his or her faith. A witness is someone who:

- lives the life of a disciple
- is willing to be known as a member of the Church
- prays for friends, neighbours and family
- takes occasional opportunities to invite people to church activities
- is able to respond to (but not necessarily initiate) questions about personal faith (see 1 Pet. 3:15)
- is able to explain the reality of God in his/her own personal life story.

Only a few believers are evangelists but *every single believer without exception* should be a witness. (John Young)

Stage 3
Discuss John Young's comments in the box (above).

In closing
Read the following statement, then pray together: 'My friend is rather shy, but she formed a bridge and Jesus Christ walked over it.'

SESSION 6: READY TO GO!

> What is especially striking is the way in which the Gospel of the Kingdom initially spread. It did not spread because of a carefully designed programme of evangelism; nor did it start because the early disciples meditated on the Great Commission and felt that they had better obey it to assuage their feelings of guilt. The Church did not begin its evangelistic activity because it was terrified about the prospects of those who died without hearing about Christ; the Christian movement was not initiated by a band of professional evangelists eager to sign up a public relations firm and get the show on the road. Rather, the Gospel spread and the Church grew because the sovereign hand of God was in the midst of the community that found itself surrounded by people who were puzzled and intrigued by what they saw happening! (Dr William Abraham)

Evangelism is primarily a divine activity, one in which God insists upon enlisting our co-operation, one in which God has chosen to work through his Church, but one which cannot be conducted without the gracious initiative and provision or equipping of God himself.

There are four essential pillars to effective evangelism:

1   *The Spirit of God*: Acts 1:5–8, Acts 2:1–13, Acts 8:26–40, Colossians 1:29.
    The Spirit is given to empower us, to direct us, to equip us, but supremely to work out the life of God in us and through us. His work is often disturbing and uncomfortable. Human beings find it next to impossible to control a strong wind; it is

much more profitable, and indeed easier, to harness its strength for positive purposes. So it is with the Spirit of God.

The Holy Spirit showers his gifts for service and ministry upon us. They are the tools of the trade for all God's servants, and we cannot manage without them.

2   *Sincere prayer*: Acts 4: 23–31, Acts 13: 1–3.

> God does nothing but in answer to prayer. (John Wesley)

> When I pray, coincidences happen. When I don't . . . they don't. (Archbishop William Temple)

> Every significant awakening in the Church has always been preceded by a concert of unusual, united, and persistent prayer. Every lessening of prayer has led, sooner or later, to a depressing sterility: the glory of the Lord rapidly departs. (Jonathan Edwards, eighteenth-century preacher)

This is one secret of the remarkable growth, vitality and vigour of so many churches in Africa, Asia and Latin America. Prayer is seen as the key to unlocking God's blessing and activity, to overcoming the kingdom of darkness, and ushering in the Kingdom of God in fuller measure.

Prayer and fasting must accompany all mission and evangelism if it is to be at all effective and powerful. Prayer and fasting go together in the Scriptures. We cannot receive anything if we are filled already. If we have our hands full, our stomachs full, our pockets full, and our calendars full, like the rich young ruler we shall not be rich at all, let alone a ruler: we shall just be poor old things. Fasting is an incarnational and sacramental expression of the first Beatitude – poverty of spirit, standing before God with our hands empty and open, waiting to receive all that is necessary for the task that he gives us to do. (Bishop Michael Marshall)

We are to pray for:
- The coming of God's Kingdom
- Christian leaders
- The witness and ministry of the Church
- Situations in which we are involved personally.

3 *Sacrificial living*: Acts 20:24.

We must be prepared to revise our own list of priorities. For we follow the one who came 'not to be served but to serve, and to give up his life as a ransom for many' (Mark 10:45).

There is a clear link in Scripture between the outpouring of God's Spirit and the obedience of God's people.

4 *A singleminded Church*: Acts 6:1–4.

The Church must take seriously the obligation to have an evangelistic edge to all its activities, to take hold of every God-given opportunity to present the Christian good news to those who have never heard, to look to the interests of the outsider in all its enterprises.

The Board of Mission (Church of England), the Christian Enquiry Agency and the Christian Publicity Organisation all have leaflets for funerals, weddings, baptisms, visitors to churches, etc., which encourage people on the edges of the Church to make one more step towards a living faith. (See p. 208.)

Our Response

This course has aimed to be thoroughly practical, to stimulate our hearts and wills as well as our minds. Our prayer is that it will bear fruit richly in our individual lives, in the life of the Church and in the wider community.

Think prayerfully and carefully for a minute or two, and write down answers to the following questions:

- What have been the one or two most significant lessons I have learned during this course?

- How am I going to put them into practice in my own Christian discipleship?
- What action should my own church/the churches together in . . . take, in order more effectively to fulfil the task of evangelism?

Finally . . .
You might want to remind yourselves of the good news.

The Bad News
For many, evangelism is a 'boo' word. It is a word of unwelcome aggravation. It signals insensitivity. It suggests charging uninvited into the deep privacy of people's lives. It conjures up images of pushy, flashy men with broad forced smiles, straight white teeth and big black Bibles. It triggers pictures of mouths without ears, emotions without reasons, confidence without questions, and religion with a price tag.

The word 'evangelism' need not conjure up any of these things. It can keep other, finer company. It could equally well remind us of the four most influential documents in the history of the world. For Matthew, Mark, Luke and John are rightly called Evangelists and their writings are rightly called Gospels.

The Good News
What is the good news that we are called to share? It is nothing less than the message of Christmas, Holy Week and Easter all rolled into one. It adds up to this: God loves us with a deep and costly love.

We live in a beautiful and exciting world. But it is an unpredictable, dangerous and sometimes terrifying world. Tragic things happen to innocent people and we are forced to ask deep questions. Do we *really* find God, truth, meaning and love at the centre of our world or are we here by sheer chance, dumped in a cold, uncaring universe?

> The good news is that God, love, truth and meaning *are* at the centre of our world. The even better news is that they can be at the centre of our individual lives, too. The best news of all is that this is not wishful thinking. It is based on evidence, on events, on widespread experience. Supremely it is rooted in a person: Jesus of Nazareth. (John Young)

Note: The following is from the funeral leaflet produced by the Board of Mission (and Christian Publicity Organisation, 01903-264556). Leaflets for a wide range of occasions are available from: Board of Mission, Church House, Great Smith Street, London SW1P 3NZ (0207-898100).

Every Funeral Is a Time of Painful Loss

The Funeral Service acknowledges this sense of grief and sorrow. But it offers hope and encouragement as well. For it speaks of the resurrection of Jesus and the reality of heaven. And it reminds us that the Lord is with us – offering strength and comfort.

This is the message which the Church has to offer you at this time.

But we know that – apart from occasions like this – many people have lost touch with the Church. We are also aware that some people are sad about this.

From time to time – and especially at a funeral – deep questions press in upon us all.

- Can we really find God, meaning and love at the centre of our universe? Or do we live in a cold, uncaring world?
- Do we live for a mere 70 or so years, only to fall off the edge into extinction? Or is there more?
- Is there a God who hears our prayers – or are we talking to ourselves?

The Christian faith does not offer glib answers to these deep questions. But it does bring confidence and hope to millions of ordinary people as they face these issues – and as they live their day to day lives.

EIGHTH COURSE

Please Listen, I'm Shouting

A Course on Listening *by Chris Woodcock, a counsellor and trainer. Chris is a member of the British Association of Counselling who works with hospice staff and prisoners. She has also worked with the Acorn Trust – whose influence on the healing ministry of the Church is immense – on courses designed to improve and refine listening skills. (See Preface and the Session which begins on p. 73.)*

The first service that one owes to others in the fellowship consists in listening to them. Just as love for God begins with listening to his Word, so the beginning of love for our friends is learning to listen to them. It is God's love for us that he not only gives us his Word but also lends us his ear. So it is his work that we do for our brothers and sisters when we learn to listen to them. (Dietrich Bonhoeffer)

This Course is not accompanied by an audio-tape. However, York Courses has produced a cassette entitled 'Struggling? Coping!'

This contains four interviews:

- Living with cancer
- Living with depression
- Living with panic attacks
- Living with loss

Further details from York Courses (for address see p. x).

SESSION 1: DEVELOPING LISTENING AND HELPING SKILLS

Exercise 1   Introductions (15 minutes)

This is designed to emphasise the importance of listening. Get into twos and introduce yourselves. Find another twosome and introduce your partner, trying to remember what he or she has told you. (No prompting!) Do this in your foursome until everyone has been introduced to the rest of the group. This should generate some fun, be a good ice-breaker and also help introduce the subject of listening straight away.

Come together as a complete group again and ask yourselves what you learned. Don't be afraid of the obvious; it can tell us a lot.

Some possible reflections may be:

- It was easy/difficult to remember the details.
- It was difficult to hear with the buzz of the other groups.
- It was interesting and I wanted to know more.
- I blanked through panic when asked to introduce my partner.

Whatever the comment or reflection, it is useful to discover some of the issues raised by 'listening' right at the beginning.

Exercise 2   Meditation (10 minutes)

A complete contrast and change of mood. The reason a time of quiet is important early in the session is to signal the importance of personal preparation. Listening is hard work.

It is even harder (and sometimes impossible) if we are full to the brim with the busyness of the day. Our minds find it hard to let go of the stuff of our own lives unless we consciously decide that, for a couple of hours at least, we will put it to one side and leave ourselves space to listen.

We are the most important tool we have, so it is essential to develop the ability to listen to our *inner* voice – as well as training ourselves for *outer* listening. We cannot do this if we are still caught up in the noise of the day. No wonder God asks us to 'be still and know . . .'

Get comfortable – all papers off laps, and take some deep breaths. Play your favourite relaxing music – a central candle to focus on may help – a poem or verse of Scripture or a gentle breathing exercise could be spoken gently over the music. The emphasis is on letting go of all your inner distractions and consciously relaxing and making inner space. It is a good idea for the leader to prepare the first meditation – carefully explaining the reasons then asking for volunteers to consider leading it in future weeks with their favourite music and/or poem.

IMPORTANT: Despite the importance of this preparation, be disciplined. Take ten minutes maximum or you will find the evening has disappeared!

Exercise 3 (10 minutes)
On your own with pencil and paper, think of a time when you wanted to talk, then consider these questions.

1 Who did you turn to and why?
2 How did you know they were listening to you? (be specific)
3 What were the qualities they offered you?
4 How did you feel?

5 Have you ever tried to talk and not been listened to?
6 How did you feel?

Now go into groups of three or four and discuss your comments for about ten minutes. (*Note to leader: it works well to mix up the groups each week so that everyone has a chance to work with everyone else.*)

What is Active Listening?

The previous exercise was designed to stimulate your understanding of listening through your own experience. Good listening is more complicated than it seems on the surface because it operates on many levels – ears, eyes, heart, brain, sensing, intuition, understanding. It is a discipline that means you consciously allow the focus of the interaction between you and your speaker to be upon the speaker. You are an essential part of that interaction and yet you must not disturb or interrupt or divert the exploration the speaker has embarked upon – you must aid it. This involves great discipline on the part of the listener. *Listening at this level is called active listening and we will be exploring and experiencing this sort of listening throughout the course.*

What did you learn from the last exercise? It is hard to pinpoint exactly how you know someone is listening to you but you certainly know if they are *not*. Perhaps you came up with examples such as 'it was the way they looked . . . they seemed interested/concerned . . . they asked the right sort of questions . . . they let me tell them all about it without interrupting me . . . they sort of smiled and nodded in the right place . . . they didn't start telling me about themselves'.

The feelings generated by such listening are always positive. On the other hand, poor listening can generate feelings of frustration, anger, sadness, lack of worth, fear (perhaps I am boring, or embarrassing my listener?).

This list of feelings emphasises just how important to our positive or negative self-image is the quality of listening we receive.

What qualities did you identify? If your listening experience was good then you will probably have experienced things like acceptance, respect, genuineness, empathy, understanding. The importance of these qualities is the foundation on which listening skills are built. If it was not good then you may have felt angry, uncared for, disregarded, made to feel small. Our sense of our own worth can be severely impaired by the lack of attention we receive from others.

Good listeners are warm, accepting people. *Who you are* is as important as *the skills you bring*. If you can balance and enhance both these aspects of listening then you will be part of an important healing process for your speaker.

Exercise 4   Listening Practice
In this final exercise it is important to:

- stay in touch with how you are feeling both as listener and speaker
- share as honestly as you can in the feedback session.

Into twos. Decide who will be speaker and who will be listener. Speaker talks on 'what brought you to this course' for up to three minutes. Remember, this is not an exercise on how well or quickly or interestingly you SPEAK. Just relax, take time to think, and enjoy your chance to be listened to. Listener, please listen WITHOUT ANY VERBAL RESPONSE. This will take a good deal of discipline, but try it and see what happens inside your head and your emotions. Now swop over. When you have finished, assemble as a group again and share your experience, first as listener, then as speaker.

- *Listener*   It is probable that at some stage you experienced a verbal response rising up within you. An opportunity to say, 'Yes – I know just what you mean,' or 'I feel exactly the same,' or 'Poor you . . .' It may have felt very false and even impolite to keep silent – or you may have found it easy! You may have discovered yourself in the middle of a conversation before you remembered that you should not be talking! You will probably have found yourself inventing many encouraging noises as a way of encouraging your speaker – or you may have found it hard to concentrate and gone walkabout inside your head!

- *Speaker*   You may have felt stuck, or that it was hard to keep going without any verbal response from your listener, or you may have relished the chance to get a few words in at last without any interruptions. You may have felt unnerved or very relaxed. Whatever your experiences, it is a valuable part of your learning to know what you, personally, found challenging and what you were able to notice about the experience both as listener and as speaker.

In the next session we will build on this experience as we look at the importance of non-verbal communication.

SESSION 2: NON-VERBAL COMMUNICATION

Exercise 1 Meditation (10 minutes)
Different members of the group may be encouraged to take responsibility for music, visual display and poem or other reading. There are many relaxation tapes available with suitable music, but anything soothing and gentle is fine. In one of my groups we had an essential oil enthusiast who brought her oil burner, a tape of panpipes and a very soothing breathing exercise. She led the session and within five minutes about fifty per cent of the group were sound asleep. It was lovely! Remember to bring it to a close after 10–12 mins or the evening will disappear. Remember also the reason for this time of quiet. Let go of the day and prepare some space inside your head and heart to listen.

Exercise 2 Non-Verbal Communication
During the meditation as you let go of the busyness of the day, you may have remembered particular feelings or emotions or experiences. If not, go over your week and see if you can identify some feelings which you or someone you had contact with experienced.

Part 1 (15 minutes)
On your own write down a list of the emotions. Now think about the emotions in terms of *facial expression* (what does it look like?), *voice tone* (what does it sound like?) and *body language* (what does it act like?), e.g.
  Emotion: Fed up.

Facial Expression: A bored or uninterested look, eyes downcast, mouth pursed, generally downcast.

Voice Tone: Flat, low, bored, monotone.

Body Language: Head tilted down, leaning, arms folded or in pockets.

Part 2 (15 minutes)

When you have identified three or four different emotions and their non-verbal expression, get into groups of three or four and discuss your lists.

Look for similarities and contrasts.

Does the group agree or disagree with the different identifications?

Discuss the importance of non-verbal communication in terms of listening.

What are the dangers of 'listening' to non-verbal communication?

Feedback (10 minutes)

Now assemble as a full group and share your insights and comments.

You may, like me, be amazed to find research indicating that up to 93 per cent of the weight of a message being communicated to another is through non-verbal communication and only 7 per cent is through verbal communication (A. Mehrabian). Think back to your session last week. What stayed with you? Probably not the actual words that were spoken to you but your experience of the group. Their friendliness (or otherwise!), their shyness perhaps, how you related to them and how they related to you. This is not to say that verbal communication was unimportant. Absolutely not. But verbal communication is always in the context of non-verbal communication and that becomes the context of the whole listening experience.

Warning

You may have already discovered in your groups that some of you had very different descriptions of the same non-verbal expression. What does this tell us? Quite simply, we may read the signals incorrectly. We can see what looks like depression (low, monotone voice tone, lack of energy, no eye contact, body in a protective shrinking pose) but it may turn out that our speaker is painfully shy. We can see red eyes, big sighs and a lot of nose blowing and assume sadness or pain but it may simply be a high pollen count! (This was my own experience and it wasn't until I was being comforted by a friend that I realised I was giving out a strong non-verbal message that I was in trouble!)

We look and listen and learn but we should **never assume**. Always hold your observations, and when the right opportunity comes, check them out. As listeners we do not have to have second sight. We sometimes misunderstand or misinterpret. No damage is done if we gently and appropriately check out our understanding with our speaker. Remember, as listeners we are always trying to communicate our understanding of our speaker's point of view. It is important, then, that we really hear all they are saying, including the non-verbal message.

People are more than the sum of their verbal and non-verbal messages.

Listening in its deepest sense means listening to clients themselves as influenced by the contexts in which they 'live, move and have their being'. (Gerard Egan)

Exercise 3   The Listener's Message (15–20 minutes)

If your speaker is giving you non-verbal messages, then remember you will be doing the same to your speaker! It is important that the messages you are giving out are the ones you want to give. Back into small groups. Discuss what messages you want to give and how, through non-verbal communication, you can give them. Think about facial expression, voice tone and body language. (Include positioning of your chairs. If you have room, take two chairs and experiment with them until you get them into what your group considers is the best position for listening.)

Feedback

Back as a whole group to share your findings. I am sure the question of eye contact came up. It is my experience that groups have many different opinions on this. There is usually a sense that it is important but concern that it is impolite to maintain a constant stare, especially when our speaker is struggling with emotion. Eye contact *is* important and, yes, staring is impolite. So how do we do it?

Think 'gentle' but be constant. As speakers struggling to express ourselves we look everywhere, but every now and then we glance back at our listener. What message would we receive if, at that very moment, our listener was looking round the room, at the clock, out of the window, into space? A very negative one. It is very important that listeners keep constant eye contact but do it gently, softly, compassionately. This is very different from the eyeball to eyeball staring that can feel very intimidating. Practise it and see! Our bodies need to be relaxed but not slouching or leaning. Legs and arms should, ideally, not be crossed (but I must admit my legs seem to do it on their own!). Be aware of this and the message it might give.

Chairs are important because they can signal power. People needing to talk are vulnerable (check out your feelings when we get to the listening exercise). If chairs are of different heights or importance (a comfortable armchair versus a stool or listener behind a desk) then issues of power/powerlessness can be introduced into the listening arena before a word has been said. The environment has a great deal of significance in establishing a therapeutic listening relationship.

I hope your group discussions touched on the question of space between the chairs, the height of the chairs, the position of the chairs. Received wisdom goes for 'ten to two' positioning. Chairs slightly turned away from each other give a more relaxed position for the body and are less threatening than a nose-to-nose type encounter.

Confidentiality is another important issue. Will you be disturbed or overheard? Is there a telephone in the room? Are there any pets or children who might interrupt? There are many things which will help to make conditions ideal, but remember the most important elements in the whole listening relationship are *you* and *your speaker*. You *can* offer valuable and focused listening in a bus queue if you have to.

Exercise 5   Listening Practice (30 minutes)
Into threes. Choose a role as listener, speaker or observer. ALL MUST HAVE A TURN AT EACH ROLE so make sure you leave time to change over. (Observer will act as time-keeper.)

- *Listener*   Listen to the **whole person**. Listen to the non-verbal communication as well as the verbal. Practise your own non-verbal communication by giving acceptance, respect and understanding through your own eye contact, body language and facial expression. Some ummms, yeses, ohhhs and other appropriate noises are permitted, but responding in words is NOT . . . yet!
- *Speaker*   Talk for up to 5 minutes on anything which has been of special interest this session. Be personal and be immediate. Speaking about a friend or a friend's opinion on something that happened last year is too distant. Speak from your experience *now* about something which touches your thoughts, feelings or behaviour.
- *Observer*   Sit out of the immediate eye-contact range. You are to be invisible to the speaker and listener but you need to be able to see and hear both of them. Take a sheet

of paper and write down what you observe. Be specific.
Look at body language, facial expression and voice tone.
Look at the non-verbal relationship between listener and
speaker and note down anything you observe. Remember
your observations are limited to what you see, not what
you imagine or analyse. The purpose is not to criticise but
to share your observations and enhance learning.

After the first listening session give feedback to each other.
Listener first, then speaker, then observer (about 5 mins).
Then swop over roles and do it all again, twice!! You will
have to be very disciplined not to chat and not to waste
valuable training time. Observer is the time-keeper and will
signal 1 minute left, however interesting the story!

Feedback
As a full group, share your experience. Comment on the different
roles in turn, describing your experience in terms of thoughts,
feelings and behaviours. Explore what it feels like in the different
roles and what you notice about yourself.

**In the next session we look at empathy and you will get to
respond verbally to your speaker!**

SESSION 3: HOW TO LISTEN WHEN IT IS DIFFICULT – PART I LISTENING SKILL – EMPATHIC RESPONDING

Exercise 1 Meditation (10 minutes)

I hope this exercise is beginning to generate its own momentum. You may have plenty of ideas and material from within the group but if not, the following meditation, spoken slowly and gently over soft music, can be very effective in this session.

Listening

When I ask you to listen to me and you start giving me advice, you have not done what I asked.

When I ask you to listen to me and you begin to tell me I shouldn't feel that way, you are trampling on my feelings.

When I ask you to listen to me and you feel you have to do something to solve my problems, you have failed me, strange as that may seem.

Listen! All I ask is that you listen. Not talk or do – just hear me.

When you do something for me that I can and need to do for myself, you contribute to my fear and weakness.

But when you accept as a simple fact that I do feel what I feel, no matter how irrational, then I can stop trying to convince you and can get back to the business of understanding what's behind this irrational feeling.

And when that's clear, the answers become obvious and I don't need advice.

Irrational feelings make sense when we understand what's behind them.

> So please listen and just hear me. And, if you want to talk,
> wait a while for your turn, and I'll listen to you. (Anon.)

Exercise 2 Listening when it is Difficult

Sometimes we find ourselves in listening situations that feel very uncomfortable. Anger and silence are two such examples. Listening to anger or silence can generate all sorts of emotions in us, and we are tempted to let our own feelings begin to take over. If that happens, the listening stops.

Anger can trigger anxiety or defensive behaviour such as being angry back, or trying to placate. Silence may tempt us into filling it inappropriately because we feel responsible or uncomfortable.

Part 1 (15–20 minutes)

Get into two groups, then decide which group will look at *anger* and which group will look at *silence*. Take a sheet of paper and write down as many things as you can think of in answer to the following questions:

1 Are there different sorts of anger/silence – and different ways of expressing them?
2 What concerns each of you about being in the presence of anger/silence? (Try to draw on personal experience.)
3 Is there anything you can do which might help? (Think what *you* would find helpful from your listener if you were expressing these emotions.)

Part 2 Feedback (10 minutes)

I hope this has focused your thinking on the listening issues presented by these difficult conditions. Present your findings to each other and be aware of any similarities or differences.

It is very important to be aware of your own fears and vulnerabilities because listening in difficult circumstances will press all your 'inner buttons'. Awareness of what is going on, both in you and in your speaker, is the first important step to being able to stay with the situation and offer active listening. You will have identified many different types of anger (explosive, frustrated, despairing, quiet . . .) and silence (peaceful, stuck, embarrassed, emotional . . .). It is important for you to know which types you find difficult. Once you know, you can be aware – and self-awareness will help you to stay with the situation without allowing your own reactive defences to change the situation.

The important question is, what might help? You may have identified a wide range of things, from putting the kettle on to trying to change the subject! The most important thing of all is *staying with your listener* – keeping the focus on her and not on your own responses. This is *active listening* and is very different from the 'Oh well, chin up, I'm sure things will work out' type of unaware listening. As you listen, try to identify the type of anger/silence you are listening to. Your best response is to express your understanding of what you see and hear, however imperfect, back to your speaker. 'I can see you are very angry.' 'It is hard for you to speak.' In this way she will feel that you are trying to enter into her experience and not trying to impose yours on her. Strange as it may seem, she will begin to hear herself.

Remember that the anger/silence you are listening to is not yours. You have not caused it to happen. Nor is it your responsibility to take it away. You are the listener. Your job is to listen and to offer as much acceptance and understanding as you genuinely can. Take the burden of the situation off your shoulders because it does not belong there. (This is very hard to do when there is silence. We seem to be pre-programmed with an 'embarrassment-buster' response which seeks to fill any spaces.) Staying with someone as an active listener when the situation becomes difficult is something that rarely happens, because our focus moves from our speaker to ourselves and shouts, 'Help! What can I do now?' *If you can stay in this situation as a listener you are offering treasure worth far more than advice or opinion.*

You are offering unconditional acceptance, respect and genuine regard. These are rare qualities which call for discipline and awareness. To listen actively to someone's anger or silence can generate a therapeutic experience no amount of words can offer. That is why it is so hard!! However, we do also need to be able to respond verbally with more than a few ummms, ahhhhs and yeses. Our response needs to be appropriate and consistent. One very effective way of doing this is called *empathic responding*.

Empathic Responding

Empathy is the foundation on which all good listening, counselling and psychotherapy rests. The importance of empathy to the listening relationship cannot be overstated. Basic empathy is the communication to another person of your understanding of their point of view with respect to experiences, behaviours and feelings. It is a skill needed throughout the listening process. Focusing on the speaker's point of view (without necessarily agreeing with it) builds a helping relationship and clarifies feelings and situations for your speaker. Empathy is variously defined as:

> Entering the private perceptual world of the other and becoming thoroughly at home in it. (Carl Rogers)

> Empathy as a form of human communication involves both listening and understanding and communicating understanding to the speaker. (Gerard Egan)

In other words, it is about *trying to see the world as your speaker sees it*. Trying to stand in their shoes and understand their feelings. And then, most importantly, being able to communicate it back. This is empathic responding.

When Fiona Castle was nursing Roy in his last months of life, she reflected on her experience:

> I felt that it was changing me, my attitude to life, to other people and particularly my ability to identify with others who are in pain or grief. I have long felt that it was impertinent to say, 'I know just how you feel, and what you are going through,' when clearly I didn't know at all. This was brought home to me at the time of my father's death, when well-

meaning friends and neighbours often failed to offer any real comfort because they couldn't really understand how I felt. (*Give Us This Day*, Kingsway, 1994)

When we are trying to understand how our speaker feels and communicate our understanding back to them we are showing empathy. We will practise this skill by:

1   Listening for 'feeling words', e.g. 'I was so *angry* at the way I had been treated', 'I felt *tired* because I didn't finish work until six', 'I was *really pleased* at the way things turned out'.
2   Using an appropriate voice tone, simply repeat back the feeling word you hear (i.e. don't change it!). E.g. 'So you were *angry* at how you had been treated', 'You were *tired* because of such a long day', 'You were *really pleased* at the way things turned out for you'.

You will notice I added the context of the feeling word when I reflected back. If you feel able, then do the same. The important thing for our practice today is to hear the feeling word and practise reflecting it back, e.g. 'you felt *angry*', 'you felt *tired*', 'you felt *really pleased*'.

Exercise 3   Listening Practice (Allow 30 mins for this)
Into threes, listener, speaker and observer.
- *Listener*   Listen out for 'feeling' words and offer them back as soon after they have been said as you can. Take care not to 're-write' the story and use an appropriate gentle and tentative voice tone. Remember the aim is to *feel* your way into your speaker's frame of reference – be gentle and remember your body language.
- *Speaker*   Pick a topic with feeling content. Perhaps something from your group work around anger or silence.
- *Observer*   Sit outside the eye contact of both listener and speaker and write down all the specific instances where a feeling word or experience is expressed by the speaker

and is, or is not, offered back through empathic responding by the listener. Notice body language and record anything interesting!

Observer is the time-keeper. Each session takes ten minutes – up to six minutes listening time and four minutes feedback.

Feedback always starts with the listener after each listening session. Focus on the process of listening rather than discussing the story. Say what you noticed about your empathic responding. Speaker, share your experience of being listened to. Observer gives specific feedback about the skills she noticed from her notes. Then swop roles until you have all had a go at everything. This is very important, because you will find a great deal of learning about listening goes on as you experience each role.

Final Feedback (5–6 minutes)
When this exercise is complete, assemble as a complete group and swop experiences as listener, speaker, and observer. Remember to protect your speaker's story – all details should remain confidential – and stick to your experience of the listening process.

Some of you may feel backed into a straitjacket with all the constraints on you as listener. It is likely that words like 'mechanical', 'too parrot-like', 'repetitive' have been expressed. You may feel silly or embarrassed at repeating back the speaker's own words. Gerard Egan points out that 'Empathy is an improbable event and is not a normal response in everyday conversations.' There is a crucial difference between chatting and active listening. As you get more accustomed to listening to feelings and experiences and offering back your empathic understanding, so you will become more and more natural in your responses. Practise at home and see what reaction you get. You may also begin to notice something about the quality of listening you are offered by others in 'everyday' life.

In the next session we will look at the skill of asking 'enabling' questions

SESSION 4: HOW TO LISTEN WHEN IT IS DIFFICULT – PART II LISTENING SKILL – 'ENABLING QUESTIONS'

Exercise 1 Meditation (10 minutes)

Remember to encourage space within by breathing out the busyness of the day, allowing your whole body and mind to relax. You may have plenty of material from within the group but if not, the following Scriptures could be used over gentle music.

> Let the wise listen and add to their learning (Prov. 1:5). Everyone should be quick to listen, slow to speak and slow to become angry (Jas. 1:19). Go near to listen rather than to offer the sacrifice of fools, who do not know that they do wrong (Eccles. 5:1). He who answers before listening – that is his folly and his shame (Prov. 18:13). He who has ears, let him hear (Matt. 11:15).

Exercise 2 Listening when it is Difficult – Part II

There are many difficult listening situations which we cannot look at in detail on this course, but following on from the previous session, here are two more particular dilemmas which constantly challenge the active listener:

1   listening to extreme emotion (grief, despair, sorrow)
2   listening to those who need answers: 'Why did this happen to me?'

Part 1 (15–20 minutes)
Use the same format as last session. Into two groups, each group choosing one of the above two situations. Debate the following questions and write down anything the group comes up with. You may have been in situations like this yourself. Anything you can share with each other from 'real life' will be very useful.

1 *Group 1:* Think of the different sorts of extreme emotions and how these may be expressed. *Group 2:* What are the questions which may be asked of you when someone is looking for answers to acute or tragic situations?
2 What concerns do you have about being with someone who is *Group 1:* expressing deep emotion; or *Group 2*: asking impossible questions?
3 Is there anything you can do which may help? (What would you value in a listener if you were in that situation?)

Part 2 Feedback (10 minutes)
When you have thoroughly explored these difficult situations and compiled your group 'answers', take turns to share them with each other including any of the real-life situations which you think appropriately illustrate your thinking.

The point of this group work is more to do with exploration than right answers. Life is messy, complicated and difficult, and of course, there are no easy, quick-fix solutions to personal dilemmas (if only!). However, there are good ways of being able to stay with someone in these difficult life crises. The emphasis is on 'stay with' rather than find a solution. Last session we practised empathic responding and I hope you remembered this as you puzzled over your dilemma.

Deep questions and difficult emotions often create a sense of embarrassment or shame for the one expressing them. (How often have I heard my speaker apologise for crying . . . how often have I heard myself do exactly the same!) Active listening promotes a sense of permission and acceptance. If your listening gives out any sense of 'this is not OK', 'I am uncomfortable with this', 'this is not good for you', then your speaker may try and squash all the emotion or questions back into the safety deposit box which lives inside. The anguish of your speaker will hide – but it will not go away.

Fiona Castle experienced this when she was coping with her husband Roy's terminal illness:

> There was one day when I was feeling really low, tired and emotionally drained. I wanted to sit down and sob, and I knew I would if anyone gave me half a chance! A friend called in to see Roy . . . He sat down for a while to talk to me, and although he asked me how I was, I found I couldn't tell him. I could only reply 'Oh, I'm fine,' which was a complete lie. I suppose I felt that I would be letting the side down if I showed any sign of strain. What I really wanted to do was cry on someone's shoulder, but perhaps deep down I felt that he couldn't have coped with that. (*Give Us This Day*)

Perhaps one of the concerns you had in your group discussions was about not being able to cope and making a difficult situation worse. If your emphasis is on trying to communicate your understanding of your speaker's distress rather than on your own desire to say the right thing and make it better, then you will not make things worse, indeed you will be supporting and offering genuine empathy. 'Getting it right' and coming up with helpful solutions to someone's distress is something we most desire to do, *but* even if our solutions worked for us it does not follow that they will work for our speaker. Everybody's situation is unique, just as every person is unique.

So what can help? Staying with the distress, staying with the questions and not being tempted into problem-solving. Be empathic. Communicate your understanding (however incomplete) by offering back the words describing their confusion or distress. Use appropriate facial expression, body language and voice tone. Remember – empathy is very different from sympathy. **Empathy** communicates understanding, *sympathy* communicates pity, however well meaning. Fiona Castle goes on to say:

> It has taught me an important lesson, that sometimes it is necessary to ask a second question, to make it clear that we are willing to hear the bad side of things, without prying or being intrusive; 'Are you feeling down today?' (*Give Us This Day*)

Fiona Castle needed to know that her listener would be able to hear her distress and would allow it. Express your acceptance and empathy by offering back what you see, i.e. 'You seem to be in such distress . . . it seems to hurt so much . . . I can see how painful this is for you.' Here the focus is on your speaker and you are responding with tentative empathy. Resist any attempt at giving your view of the situation, as in 'If I were you, I would . . .' 'What you need is . . .' These responses all bring the focus on to you, the listener, and your opinion.

It is the same principle with questions. The empathic response to 'Why has this happened to me?' is 'You are looking for answers to why this has happened to you.' The empathic response to 'Where is God in all this?' is 'You are trying to make sense of your faith in all this.' *The answer to the impossible question is an empathic statement which communicates the anguish of the question rather than looks for a solution to the question. Nobody has the answer to suffering.*

On the printed page, these responses can seem contrived or cold. Used in context with genuine warmth and a willingness to be with your speaker whatever emotional storm or impossible questions they are struggling with, they become an invaluable part of the healing process.

Exercise 3   Enabling Questions (10–15 minutes)
Into twos, quickly ask each other a question (any question)
and write these down. See what you can observe about the
question you asked and the answer it evoked. Discuss with
each other what are the positive aspects of asking questions
and what might be the negative ones. Jot down the central
points of your discussion and then assemble as a whole
group.

Open and Closed Questions
The skill of asking enabling questions is all about encouraging
your speaker to talk more freely, to open up the subject rather than
close it down. (Some of you will have experienced coming to a
halt in previous listening sessions when your listener was forbidden
to respond to you.) It is important, therefore, to ask *open questions*
rather than *closed questions*. An open question literally has an open
end which the speaker can then expand: e.g. 'What sort of a day
have you had today?' It invites any number of responses, therefore
it is an open question; 'Have you had a good day?' invites a yes or
no response and is a closed question.

Positive Aspects of Asking Questions
Questions can enable a speaker to fully explore the situation and
the feelings associated with it. Be alert to the emotional content
of the story and use your questions to open up this area, e.g. 'So
what are your feelings about that . . . ?' or 'Can you say how you
feel . . . ?' If your speaker begins to struggle or dry up and you
sense the silence is a 'stuck' one, then a simple question like 'Can
you tell me any more about this situation?' or 'Is there anything
else you would like to say about this?' or 'What was that like for
you?' can help your speaker to focus back on what they are
exploring.

> Go back into your pairs and identify what sort of question
> you asked. If it was a closed question, try reframing it to
> make it open. (5 mins)

Negative Aspects of Asking Questions

Too many questions can create a sense of interrogation and will
result in your speaker closing down. Questions asked for the sake
of curiosity are neither respectful nor empathic. (Notice your inner
curiosity – we all have it! – but hold it and remain focused on
enabling your speaker to explore what is helpful for them.)

Asking questions when your speaker is full of emotion tends to
deflect the emotion and can give an unspoken, 'It is not all right
for you to be emotional' signal. Multiple questions (the mistake I
often make) are often the result of trying to get the question right.
Asking it in three or four different ways without giving the speaker
a chance to answer, can result in confusion for both of you.

The main points to remember about asking enabling questions
are:

1 Ask an open question.
2 Use a tentative, gentle, exploratory voice tone. A one–word
   empathic reflection said with an upward questioning lilt is an
   excellent way of asking an enabling question.
3 Stay empathic, so that all questions enable the speaker to say
   more about what they are already saying. Questions should
   never deflect from the story because of curiosity.
4 Never ask WHY? Why questions can sound judgemental and
   critical. 'Why did you do that?' 'Why do you want to run
   away?' Most of us do not know why. A better way is to ask
   WHAT? E.g. 'What was happening for you?' 'What is it about
   your situation that makes you feel like running away?'

Finally: **_don't panic_**, even if you find yourself asking closed
questions / multiple questions / poorly timed questions / why
questions. Just notice what you are doing, adjust accordingly and

keep listening to your speaker. If you do everything 'wrong' yet you sincerely endeavour to listen closely to your speaker, you will be offering something of value.

Exercise 4   Listening Practice (45 minutes in total)
Take up to ten minutes each to explore your topic. At the end of each session give three minutes feedback starting with the listener, then speaker then observer. Beware of analysing the story. Stick with the listening process and be specific about your use of the skills and how you experienced them.

- *Listener*   Ask 'enabling questions'. Remember to listen to the body language and to use empathic responding for all feeling words. If your speaker does not tell you how she feels, use your enabling questions to find out!
- *Speaker*   Use a topic from the group work that has struck a particular chord with you. Or choose any recent life event that has 'feeling' content. The only requirement is that it is real and it 'belongs' to you.
- *Observer*   Stay out of the eye-contact line of listener and speaker. Write down what sort of questions are asked and what the response is. Also note any empathic responses and notice body language. Observer is responsible for timing so warn your speaker when there is 1 minute left, so the session can be drawn to a close. It is important you leave enough time for each of you to experience each role.

Although it sounds daunting, you will be surprised at your own expertise if you can allow yourself to focus gently but empathically on your speaker.

Feedback
After you have each taken a turn and given feedback to each other, come together as a whole group and share your experiences. Valuable learning will come out of all these situations, whether

you were able to do them 'copy-book' style – or managed to tie yourself up in knots! Notice what you did *right* as well as what you did *wrong*. Remember to guard your speaker's story (confidentiality is vital) and stick to discussing the *process* rather than *content*. Do not be tempted to speak for anyone else – unless you want to praise them, of course!

In the next session we will be practising the skill of summarising.

SESSION 5: MY BIGGEST RESOURCE IS ME – SUMMARISING

Exercise 1 Meditation (10 minutes)

Suggestion: Use this time to give yourself some TLC (Tender Loving Care). With gentle music as a background, the leader encourages the group to imagine all the excess luggage they have brought with them to the group. Imagine how many bags and how big they are. Then begin to unpack them. See what you are carrying around that you would rather put in the bin or skip (there may be a lot!). See what situations or feelings or physical aches and pains are in your luggage. Ask yourself what you would like to ditch and what you would like to shelve for the time being and then mentally do it. Put all the things you would like to be rid of in your mental dustbin and all the things which may be a distraction to you under your chair until the end of your session. Then take some deep breaths and see if you can feel the difference.

Exercise 2 (Allow up to 30 minutes)

Step 1 (5 minutes)

On your own with paper and pen:

1 List three adjectives which would describe someone you like or admire.
2 Now list three or four (and more if you can) strengths and positive qualities which *you* possess.

Many people struggle with expressing their own strengths. If you are finding it hard, think about the compliments you have received: e.g. you are patient, caring, a good listener, a good cook, organised, enthusiastic, determined, cheerful . . .

Step 2 (15 minutes)
Get into groups of three.

1 Take turns to share your positive qualities with the group. Group to encourage non-verbally, then one of the group uses empathic responding to reflect back each positive quality. Group to listen out for any negative elements creeping into the positive list ('I am a very patient person **but** . . . ') and challenge this firmly. No 'buts' are allowed!
2 When you have all shared your positive qualities with each other, begin to explore the barriers which make it hard to express positive personal qualities, and write them down.
3 Now look at the three adjectives which you have used to describe someone you admire. Explore to what extent **you** possess these.

Step 3 (10 minutes)
As a complete group, share with each other what you have come up with in your threesomes. This can be a very hard exercise. If you were asked to list everything you were **dis**satisfied with about yourself you may have found it easier! It is very important that we appreciate our own good qualities if we are to be empathic with others. **Your biggest resource as a good listener is yourself.**

You are unique, and if you are able to give the whole of yourself to a listening encounter then your speaker will feel valued, worthwhile and esteemed. It is hard to do this if you undervalue yourself. Know that when you give yourself you give something of value.

The barriers which make it hard for us to value ourselves are many. Culturally, the British do not go in for self-congratulation. We often believe that our faith tells us always to consider others

and not ourselves, and forget that we are told to 'love our neighbours *as ourselves*'. There can be a sense of shame or embarrassment
in giving ourselves due appreciation, and this can come from our
early training. Passive self-sacrificing behaviour was often praised
and encouraged at school and at home, and this can lead to the
belief that it is what we *do* for others that is of value, not ourselves.

You may have come up with other reasons as to why it is hard
for us to value ourselves, but I hope you can feel a sense of
achievement in having identified and expressed some of your own
strengths and qualities.

You may or may not have been able to see yourself in the
positive qualities you gave to someone you admire, but it is
interesting to see how often it is the case that there are some
similarities when you allow yourself to look for them.

Developing the skill of summarising

Being able to give your speaker a summary of what they have
already said is a very useful skill, but it calls for careful listening.
'Summary' is literally the sum of the parts. It brings together the
main points of the speaker's story, in terms of content and feeling.
It can further the speaker's exploration of their story and can enable
them to gain greater understanding of their problems. In turn this
enables the listener to encourage the speaker to move forward.

All this just by offering back what the client has just told you!
Remember, you do not have to offer deep wisdom and insight
into the speaker's story. *What you are required to do is to listen*.
Listen very carefully. Listen to the content and the feelings. Then
at various points throughout the story, and most especially at the
end, offer back a mini summary.

Summarising helps to clarify the situation when the story is
complex, or when it is presented with some confusion. Stories
rarely come out in simple linear form. We struggle to understand
our feelings and can get lost in what we are trying to say. A good
listener will respond with empathy, will ask enabling open
questions, and will offer mini summaries in order that both she and
the speaker can explore the situation and try to make some sense of
the disorder.

It is very important that all the elements of your summary come from the speaker's own words. Do not add to the summary by giving your own opinion or your own insight. Be disciplined with this and ask yourself where your focus is. If it is on your speaker then you will be listening to all she has to say, both verbally and non-verbally. If it is on you, then you will be trying to work out what on earth you can say in this situation. Remember to use the speaker's own story, the speaker's own words and the speaker's own feelings. If there is silence, listen to it. If you feel lost and confused, **don't panic**. Ask your speaker to give **you** a summary of where she is in all this. It is all right to be yourself. One of the most important elements of the listening relationship is what you can bring in terms of empathic understanding, acceptance, genuineness and sincerity.

You do not *have to be the wise person with wise words*. **You do** *have to be genuinely committed to listening to your speaker, and that means checking out your own understanding frequently*.

When you go to your listening practice, you will listen to *both* the verbal and non-verbal story. You will listen for 'feeling' words and reflect them back empathically. You will ask enabling questions which help the speaker to explore more fully their story ('. . . and what was that like for you?' 'Can you say a little more about that?' 'What are your feelings about this situation?'). You will also offer a summary at points throughout the story and, as a way of bringing the listening to a close, right at the end.

It does sound daunting, but have a go and remember these simple points.

1   Clear away the thoughts you have brought with you.
2   Focus your attention on the speaker.
3   Hear what is said.
4   Check your understanding frequently.
5   Pick up key words and feelings and reflect back, frequently.
6   Summarise main themes.

Exercise 3   Listening Practice (40–45 minutes)
Take up to 10 minutes each for your listening practice and 3
minutes each for feedback.

- *Listener*   Relax and listen – use all the skills you
  have acquired and be aware that your biggest resource is
  you.
- *Speaker*   Pick a topic based on your feelings or experiences in the previous exercise on the difficulties or otherwise in identifying your own strengths and qualities. Please
  do not feel you have to take a deep breath and somehow
  speak non-stop for 10 minutes. This is not a test on
  speaking! Use your time to explore your feelings. You
  have a listener who is devoted to your every word, so
  relax and enjoy the undivided attention.
- *Observer*   You will need to work hard at noticing all the
  listening elements being practised today. Write down
  specific interventions, i.e. feeling words reflected back,
  enabling questions asked, summaries offered. Try to notice
  the effect of these interventions on the listening relationship and jot down what you see. Observer acts as time-
  keeper. Do a brief feedback after each listening session,
  then swop roles.

Feedback (10 minutes)
This is hard work, isn't it! I hope you have begun to experience
the complementary way in which these skills build upon each
other. They are designed to allow you to focus all your energy on
helping the speaker hear and explore and clarify their stories. It is
from this that insight and decisions can come.

As a whole group, assess your experiences as listener, speaker and observer in turn. Each role will have something to teach you about listening skills. Your own experience in each role, however easy or difficult, will have something to teach the rest of the group. My hope is that some of you will have begun to experience the joy and privilege of offering your speaker, genuine active listening.

In our final session we will focus on our 'journey'.

SESSION 6: THE JOURNEY

Note to leaders: Please note the need for paper and felt-tip pens.

Exercise 1   Meditation (10 minutes)

The last session in this series has as its theme the journey. Everyone is on a journey through life, and your group has for a brief time come together to journey through the world of listening. As a final meditation you may have a favourite poem or story with a journey as a theme. If not, the following piece is called *The Center* (Anthony de Mello, Wellsprings, 1984), and the journey it describes is the journey within.

> Imagine that you walk into a safe and tranquil place, a
>   special place for you.
> Spend some time exploring the surroundings,
>   then settle down to contemplate your life.
>
> See how frequently you rush outside yourself – to
>   people, occupations,
> places, things – in search of strength and peace and
>   meaning,
> forgetting that the source of all is here within your own
>   heart.
> It is here that you must search.
>
> Each person carries thoughts that have the power to
>   being peace.
> Let us search for ours.
> Search also for the thoughts that help you face life's
>   challenges
>   with fortitude and courage.

What are the thoughts that make you warm and gentle,
that counteract the anger or bitterness in your heart?
What are the thoughts that put meaning in your life?
Produce contentment?
Give you joy?
Propel you into service?

Pause for several minutes for the group to meditate on these questions.

We must now prepare to leave this special place but
before we go
Let us recall the existence of another source within
That does not need the aid of thoughts
to give us all we need.

Imagine a cave within your heart suffused with light.
The light invades your body as you enter.
You can feel its rays create and energise and warm and
heal.

Let us sit within the cave in silent adoration
as the light seeps in through every pore.

Stay with the silence for a few minutes, then gently encourage
the group to begin to be aware of their surroundings and of
the group, and slowly to journey back into awareness.

Exercise 2   Personal Journey (30 minutes)

As listeners trying to make space and time in a busy world to
share the journey of those who need a listening ear, it is
important that we have space and time to reflect on aspects of
our own journey. Our exercise today is to draw a part of our
own journey and you will need a large sheet of paper (flip-

chart paper or the reverse side of wallpaper!) and lots of coloured felt-tip pens.

Take time to decide what timescale you want to represent, and choose a period which has significance for you. You could take an overview and choose from birth to the present, marking down all the significant events, both good and bad, as though they were signposts on your own personal road. Or you may want to choose the weeks you have been on this course and draw some of your learning experiences and how they have fitted into your life – or otherwise! You may want to take a slice of time representing a few significant years or months that you feel drawn to reflect upon.

Remember, this exercise is about exploring and reflecting on journeys which have brought you to this place in your life, at this point in time.

When I say 'draw', I use the term loosely! Stick figures, symbols and squiggles are all fine so long as you know what they represent. It is useful to have in mind the metaphor of a journey, so you may want to draw a long and winding road, or river, or railway track, or . . . whatever your imagination comes up with to represent the passage of time. Along the route there may have been 'mountains' to climb, 'rivers' to cross, 'cul-de-sacs' to detain you. These may represent joyful celebrations or times of real struggle.

Find your own space with your drawing materials. Take a deep breath and put your inhibitions in your mental dustbin! You have up to half an hour for this, so take your time and let your pictorial journey develop.

Exercise 3   Feedback (10 minutes)

Come together as a whole group, without your pictures, and discuss the *process* of drawing your journey rather than the *content* of your journey. What was it like trying to decide what timescale to choose? What was it like having to go back to 'nursery school' and draw a big picture? Were there any surprises for you that began to develop out of your reflections? Did you feel it was an impossible task? What other feelings were you aware of?

As listeners we need to be very aware that, for our speakers, reflecting and speaking about their 'journey' may be difficult and may evoke thoughts, feelings and behaviours ranging from tremendous relief to a sense that this is a 'silly' or 'embarrassing' thing to do. As you drew your journey, it may be that you also felt some of these things. This is very useful learning and will help your empathic responses.

Exercise 4   Listening Practice (30 minutes)

Now find a partner and take turns (15 minutes each) using your listening skills, to help your partner explore their drawing and talk over their journey with you.

- *Listener*   Stay empathic and reflect any feeling words. Use enabling questions to help the speaker explain and explore their journey. Use positive non-verbal communication to encourage further explanation and stay sensitive to the possibility of difficult areas. Summarise frequently and finish with a summary of the main elements of the story.
- *Speaker*   Use this opportunity to explore your inner reflections, represented by your picture. Take time to look and think and feel. Your listener is there to help you explore and talk about the things you choose to say.

There is no observer for this final exercise, so try and stay aware of time constraints. You will need 12 minutes each as speaker with a brief feedback before you swop roles.

Exercise 5   Final Evaluation and Feedback
Listening
Come back together as a whole group for the final time and share with each other what it was like for you as *listener* with the added dimension of a drawing. Did you notice anything about your skills? Is it getting more comfortable to use empathic responding and ask enabling questions? Were you able to summarise? Are you still listening to non-verbal messages? I hope you are able to give yourself a pat on the back where it is deserved as well as express your frustration when you notice your areas for development.

Speaking
As *speaker*, share what it was like to explore a part of yourself and your life using your drawing. In what ways did you find your listener helpful?

As a final evaluation it may be useful for you to try to summarise what you feel have been the main areas of learning for you from the entire course. Write it down on paper and either take turns to share each evaluation in the whole group or split into a final threesome and share it there.

Most of the training courses I have led have ended with a celebration involving food and drink, so you may want to organise something that will suit your group and be a fitting way of ending this part of your listening journey. But whatever you do, don't forget to give yourselves, and each other, and your leader, an emphatic WELL DONE for having completed the course!

Also by John Young

The Case Against Christ

In this bestselling book, John Young acts as counsel for the defence in the case against Christ and invites atheists, agnostics and enquirers to join the lively debate. Material for group discussion is also included.

'*A Classic.*' CHURCH PASTORAL AID SOCIETY

'*If ministers will put this book to use among all the members of their congregations, the result will be many less defensive Christians, better able to cope with the usual charges against their position.*'
CHURCH OF ENGLAND NEWSPAPER

'*Quite first class.*' BISHOP HUGH MONTEFIORE

Hodder & Stoughton
ISBN 0 340 52462 6

Know Your Faith

The excitement of Christian truth presented afresh in an eight-week study of the Apostles' Creed. This book is designed for individual readers and for discussion groups.

'*A major resource.*' GEORGE CAREY,
THE ARCHBISHOP OF CANTERBURY

'*John Young has a great gift for communicating profound ideas simply and readably.*' JOHN HABGOOD, FORMER ARCHBISHOP OF YORK

'*An excellent course.*' BRIAN HOARE,
PAST PRESIDENT OF THE METHODIST CONFERENCE

Hodder & Stoughton
ISBN 0 340 54487 2